The
New England
Guest House
Book

Library of Congress Cataloging in Publication Data
Ross, Corinne Madden.
  The New England guest house book

  Includes index.
  1. Hotels, taverns, etc.—New England—Directories. I. Title.
TX907.R588 1982   647'.9474   81-17341
ISBN 0-914788-54-X   AACR2

Cover design by Talmadge Moose.
Inside illustrations provided by the guest houses of New England.
Typography by Raven Type.

East Woods Press Books
Fast & McMillan Publishers, Inc.
429 East Boulevard
Charlotte, N.C. 28203

The New England Guest House Book

Corinne Madden Ross

The East Woods Press

Table of Contents

For my mother.

Introduction

Travelers in Great Britain and Europe have long been familiar with the popular form of lodgings called "Bed and Breakfast." In the United States, a similar type of accommodations has been available for many years—the guest house, sometimes called a tourist home. Until recently, however, American guest houses have remained pretty much a well-kept secret shared only by experienced travelers and those fortunate enough to come upon them by chance.

Today the situation is changing. Not only are more people discovering the pleasures of staying at a guest house, but the number of houses—which only a few years ago was waning —is now on the increase. And many of their proprietors are practicing the hospitable European custom of offering breakfast to their guests. Of the 186 guest houses described in this edition of **The New England Guest House Book** almost two-thirds do provide breakfast, included in the rates or for a small extra charge. Some of the others offer complimentary wake-up coffee and juice.

If you have never stayed at one, perhaps you're wondering what a guest house is, exactly. It is not an inn, despite the fact that many houses call themselves "inns." A true inn is a public lodging place that includes a full-service restaurant and usually a lounge or bar. A guest house, generally, is smaller than an inn, and is a private home whose owners offer lodging only or lodging plus breakfast. Guest house proprietors who use the word "inn" do so, they say, because they feel it conveys the sense of warmth and old-fashioned hospitality most people associate with inns. But a guest house, no matter what it is called, also offers just those admirable qualities.

Another pleasing attribute of guest houses is their cost. Rates are generally amazingly modest; even in high-priced resort areas the rates are usually far lower than those of most motels or hotels. Guest houses are ideal for families, too. Most welcome children; owners often provide cots or rollaways for a small fee, and there is almost always a spacious yard where youngsters can play.

9

The greatest charm of guest houses, however, lies in their surprising individuality—a refreshing change from the impersonal monotony of most motel accommodations. In New England, their ranks include some of the region's loveliest old homes, often centuries old ... with fascinating histories and a gratifying diversity of architectural styles. You may stay in a sea captain's historic Colonial home dating back to the 18th century, or an elegant Federal or Victorian mansion. Other guest houses include cozy old farmhouses, contemporary chalets in the mountains, and beach cottages large and small. Some are just comfortable, unassuming homes of no particular distinction.

Their interiors may be grand or quite plain. Antiques abound in the older houses, including four-poster beds, marble-topped tables or dressers and handmade quilts. Ceilings are high and the rooms are large and airy. Polished wood and gleaming spotlessness are the norm, even in the simplest houses.

Guest houses are relaxing, friendly places, often with broad porches, lawns and lovely gardens which the guest is encouraged to use. Indoors there may be a delightful old kitchen where travelers are served morning coffee and homemade muffins—or a pleasant sitting room with a fireplace to gather around in winter months, and perhaps a piano for sing-a-longs. Books, magazines, games and television are usually available for guests to enjoy for rainy days or for evening entertainment.

Fresh flowers in your room are often another of the graceful personal touches that make the guest house an especially inviting place to stay. Some proprietors serve afternoon tea, indoors or out in the garden. In many houses, the guests are welcome to make tea or coffee at any hour; a few offer kitchen privileges. And you are free to come and go as you wish, just as though you were visiting an old acquaintance.

Guest house owners are all different types: grandmotherly ladies, young couples and older ones, families, and single men and women of all ages. The majority seem to have one thing in common—they truly enjoy meeting people and making friends with their guests. Your hosts will be delighted to direct you to the best places to eat and shop in the vicinity, and offer helpful suggestions on things to see or do, such as country fairs or a bean supper in a nearby church. Some proprietors act as concierges, making dinner reservations for guests at local restaurants, or arranging tours of the area.

You may have just as much privacy as you desire in a guest house, and the walls are generally thicker than in a motel. But please do give your fellow guests a chance; you may very well find yourself forming some lasting friendships. Guests are just as varied as the owners and their houses—professional people, vacationers with or without families, skiers, hikers and hunters. Many European travelers choose to stay at guest houses. They often prefer them to any other form of lodging not only because they are accustomed to the economical bed and breakfast idea, but because guest houses offer the authentic "feel" of a region.

As a rule, guest houses are conveniently located in or near a town; visitors can easily walk to restaurants, antique or gift shops, museums, beaches and other local points of interest. Parking is generally provided on the premises or nearby. Even if you come without a car you'll be able to get around without effort. Some thoughtful guest house owners will arrange to meet you at the bus stop, train station or airport. In many towns, bicycles, mopeds, canoes, sailboats and motorboats are available for rental.

There are, of course, some travelers who would find a guest house lacking in certain amenities. Some people feel deprived without an ice machine down the hall, a telephone and television set in each room, and room service. Air conditioning is uncommon, but most regions of New England don't need it. Also, one must share a bathroom in many of the houses, although private baths are often available. Few guests, however, feel that sharing a bath is a hardship. Fresh towels and soap are always provided.

As most guest houses are small with only a few rooms available for travelers, making reservations in advance by phone or letter is a good idea—and sometimes required. Some guest houses also request an advance deposit; a few ask for a minimum stay of two or three days, especially over holiday weekends. Credit cards are not usually accepted; cash or traveler's checks are preferred. Personal checks are often acceptable, but it's advisable to ask ahead of time.

Because rates, like everything else nowadays, tend to increase from time to time, I have not listed specific prices. Instead, the house's rates (for double occupancy) are described as falling into one of three general categories:

```
Inexpensive  . . . . . . . . . . . . . . .($10-$25)
Moderate  . . . . . . . . . . . . . . . .($25-$45)
Expensive  . . . . . . . . . . . . . . . .($45-up)
```

One further note: many guest houses will allow one or more extra persons to share a room for a small added charge.

A large number of guest houses stay open year-round but some, especially in seaside areas, close for the winter. Others may close for a vacation for a month or so in early spring. Information on dates open has been included for each house. If the guest house is a bed and breakfast establishment it has been so noted, with a description of the food served. The index also indicates which houses serve breakfast, with a star next to their names. Usually the meal is a simple continental breakfast; some proprietors provide full breakfasts. A few also offer lunch or dinner, but the meals are usually optional or by reservation, and are generally served only during the off season when many of the local restaurants are closed.

As some towns in New England are dry, you might want to bring along your own supply of something spirited, or buy it along the way. Your host or hostess can probably be persuaded to provide an ice cube or two, and sometimes a refrigerator will be available for keeping soft drinks, beer, wine and perishables.

I have not attempted to list each and every guest house in New England. Instead, I have tried to present a sampling of typical houses located in regions most visited by tourists as well as in some not-so-familiar areas. In towns with many guest houses, the traveler is given the pleasant choice of deciding which one sounds most appealing. If you find yourself in a town not mentioned in the book, keep your eyes open for a house beside the road with the sign "Guests." In addition, the local Chamber of Commerce or tourist information headquarters may be able to suggest a guest house in the vicinity.

The descriptions of the houses included in this book are as accurate as possible. Sometimes, however, situations and/or owners change, and if you should find any of the accommodations not living up to your expectations I would very much appreciate your letting me know. Also, as you travel, if you discover a guest house that you think would make a good addition, write to me about it so that it can be considered for inclusion in the next edition.

A good rule of thumb to use in searching out a new and unfamiliar guest house—or any guest house, for that matter—is to decide if you like its looks from the road. If you do, it's likely you will find it just as attractive inside. Good proprietors take as much pride in maintaining their yards as they do their houses. And if you have any doubts at all, ask to see the house before you settle in; the owner will be more than happy to show you around. If the house is not filled, you probably will have the choice of several rooms varying in size.

New England is a remarkably beautiful region, visited by travelers from all over the world. Its six states are similar in many ways, yet each has its distinct differences. They are all rich in history, cultural and sports activities, and spectacular scenery. Excellent highways crisscross every state, fine for reaching a destination rapidly. But the best way to discover New England is to follow the secondary routes and back roads, by car or bicycle. Just remember that though distances look short on the map, the roads are very winding and often narrow. So allow plenty of time to get wherever you're going—besides, you'll probably want to stop and explore along the way.

These scenic byways will take you through tiny Colonial villages, inland valleys and forested wilderness areas; past vine-covered stone walls, sparkling lakes and tumbling streams; over rugged mountain passes; along broad beaches and a jagged, rockbound seacoast. They will also lead you to the delightful guest houses of New England, where you are cordially invited to linger . . . and get to know both the region and its people.

The Carriage House Inn, Searsport, Maine

The Captain Lord Mansion, Kennebunkport, Maine

Maine

Evergreen trees, their thickly-needled tips stabbing upwards against the horizon—these are the very essence of Maine. Its nickname, fittingly, is "The Pine Tree State." Vast tracts of dark-green forests, mostly owned by paper and lumber companies, cover more than four-fifths of the land. Pointed firs march in massed ranks all the way down to the ocean's edge, somehow managing to thrive atop the tumbled granite ledges that form Maine's incredible coastline.

It is the seacoast that attracts the majority of visitors to New England's (and the country's) northeasternmost state. U.S. Rte. 1 follows the coast—sort of. To actually *see* the coast of Maine, however, the traveler must work at it. If a straight line were drawn directly up the seaboard, the distance covered would be only 228 miles. But when the actual shoreline is measured, including the off-lying islands, the distance is 3478 miles!

You can't just merrily bowl along in your car and expect to be awed by splendid vistas of sea and rock. They're there, all right. But many of them can be reached only by making a sideways trek eastward from Rte. 1, in some cases for a good many miles. You must study your map, and then decide which of the innumerable capes, coves, and long, narrow peninsulas you wish to explore.

Millions of years ago the mighty peaks of a gigantic mountain range loomed along this coast. During the Ice Age, massive glaciers ground down the mountains, allowing the ocean to rush in. When the glaciers were gone, they left behind one of the most ragged seacoasts in the world. The offshore islands—hundreds and hundreds of them—are the tops of some of those drowned mountains.

In the early 1600s the French and English founded small settlements along the coast, both of which failed. The English Popham Colony, near the mouth of the Kennebec River, was abandoned after one bitter Maine winter; the colonists informed the Mother Country that no one could ever survive in that climate. Some modern-day State of Mainers claim to agree with this opinion, and spend their winters in Florida if they can manage it.

Most of the inhabitants, however, relish the colder months with their clear, crisp air, and the return to leisurely, slow-paced living. Snug harbors are emptied of their summertime jams of pleasure craft; only the fishing boats remain. An atmosphere of serenity pervades the coastal villages. Snow drifts quietly down upon beaches and gray rock, clinging to tree branches and piles of lobster pots.

Many guest houses close in late September or mid-October for winter, but a few remain open year-round. Those that do provide the off-season visitor with a unique opportunity to experience the timeless quality of everyday life in a small Maine village. For a growing number of travelers, this is the best time of all to come. There's not as much activity, perhaps, but winter's dazzling beauty, and the joy of having it all to yourself, are more than enough enticement for most people.

In summer, the seacoast swarms with tourists, and guest houses galore are there for the choosing. The sun doesn't always shine, of course. Rain falls occasionally. Some days fog rolls softly in from the sea, but that's part of being near the ocean. A walk along the sands or rocks in swirling salt-mist, all sound muffled except for the constant boom of the surf, can become an unforgettable memory. Activities are available to suit every taste and all forms of weather: antiquing, sightseeing, clambakes, boat trips to the islands, seal-watching, rock-crawling, exploring tidal pools, and swimming—even though the ocean *is* a tad too invigorating for comfort.

Strike up a conversation with the local inhabitants whenever possible. Maine folk are proud, direct, and—despite their reputed taciturnity—downright chatty when given a chance. Don't attempt to imitate the delightfully twangy accent, though. You will only amuse the natives, and run the risk of earning the derisive sobriquet, "summer complaint."

Heading north up the coast (or "down" the coast to those in the know) you'll find a profusion of charming towns, villages, and seaside resort areas. The most popular are York Beach, Ogunquit, Kennebunkport, Old Orchard Beach and Boothbay Harbor, all within an easy drive from Boston. Further "downeast" are Rockport, Camden and Searsport, and then

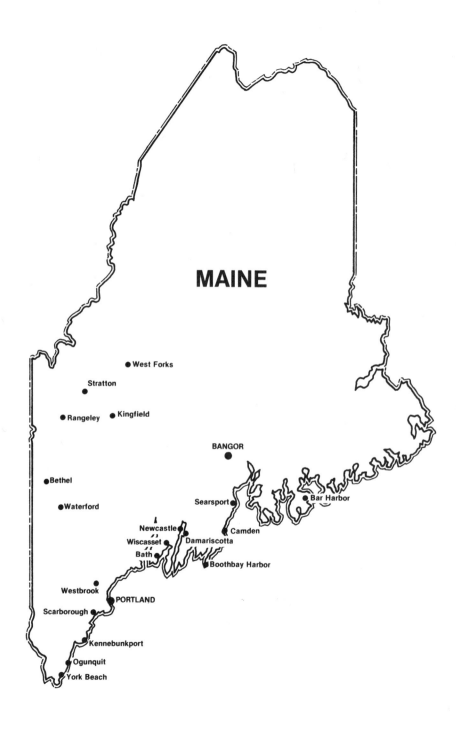

MAINE

West Forks

Stratton

Rangeley   Kingfield

BANGOR

Bethel

Waterford   Searsport   Bar Harbor

Newcastle   Camden
Wiscasset   Damariscotta
Bath
            Boothbay Harbor

Westbrook

PORTLAND

Scarborough

Kennebunkport

Ogunquit

York Beach

Guest Houses

the grand old summer watering place of the wealthy, Bar Harbor, near spectacular Acadia National Park.

Intrepid travelers may journey onwards to the nation's easternmost point, Quoddy Head State Park in Lubec, across Passamaquoddy Bay from New Brunswick, Canada. A bridge takes you out to Campobello Island, where Franklin D. Roosevelt had his summer home. And for those with an insatiable urge to see what comes next, there is Aroostook County, way, way north . . . home of the famed Maine potato.

Inland, Maine offers some 2500 lakes. Its topography ranges from gently rolling countryside to mountains, and uninhabited wilderness areas slashed by whitewater rivers. Hiking, canoeing, rafting, swimming and fishing are some of the many summertime things to do. For winter travelers there are ski resorts, mostly located in the central and western sections nearing the New Hampshire border. Less athletic visitors can enjoy cross-country skiing, snowshoeing, and the simple pleasure of just getting away from city tensions and polluted air.

Forestry, fishing and tourism are the state's major industries. In addition, tons of potatoes are harvested annually, and prodigious crops of blueberries. Maine has a well-deserved reputation for good food: blueberry pie and the incomparable just-out-of-the-ocean lobster are only two of the region's specialties.

THE YORKS

The southernmost tourist area on Maine's seacoast is known as the Yorks—York Village, York Harbor and York Beach—all on Rte. 1A. York Village, originally called Agamenticus, was settled in 1624. It was incorporated in 1642 as Gorgeana, named after Sir Ferdinando Gorges, English soldier and mariner, then proprietor of the Province of Maine. Known as the first English "city" in America, Gorgeana was seized by Massachusetts in 1652 along with the rest of the province. It was reduced to a town, and renamed York.

Hostile Indians frequently attacked the town, almost destroying it in 1692, killing or capturing about half of the inhabitants. York Village today is a living museum with its beautiful old buildings preserved as they were in Colonial days. Old Snowshoe Rock, where the Abenakis were supposed to have left their snowshoes before their deadly raid, is one of the area's many interesting historical sites. The Old Gaol

18

Museum, known as the King's prison, is noted for its gloomy dungeons and fine collections of china and furniture.

Four magnificent beaches and a deep, landlocked harbor provide surf and deep sea fishing, boating and swimming, including a tidal pool for children. Scenic Nubble Light on Cape Neddick is popular for picnicking, photo-taking and rock-climbing.

Nirvana By-the-Sea. Directly above the ocean near Nubble Light, Nirvana By-the-Sea offers guests salt-tanged air and the ever-present sound of the surf. A typical comfortable New England beach house, all of its six guest rooms have a marvelous view of the sea below; most have their own private terraces. There's also a kitchenette apartment for rental. A patio down on the rocks overlooking the Atlantic has an outdoor fireplace for lobster cookouts, and there's a screened summer house. Mr. and Mrs. Francis T. Murphy provide freshly-perked hot coffee in the morning. Guests may use the fully-equipped kitchen or walk to one of the nearby restaurants for meals. *Nubble Road, York Beach, ME 03910; (207) 363-3628. (Just past York Beach on Rte. 1A, take a right on Nubble Road. It's a gray, red-roofed house on the right, a bit less than a mile.) Rates are moderate. Open May 30-October.*

Jo-Mar's Guest House. An attractive house on a quiet street, Jo-Mar's sits on a bluff above Short Sands Beach and Nubble Peninsula. The view is spectacular, especially from the landscaped terrace overlooking cliffs and ocean. The house, a cross between Colonial and mid-Victorian architecture, was originally a summer boardinghouse for female telephone company employees. Supposedly a "guardian angel" resides in the attic; he (or she) has helped bring the structure safely through several violent winter storms without a speck of damage! Formerly a guest house called The Emerald Sea, Jo-Mar's has been renamed for its new proprietors, Joan Curtis and her mother, Mary Della Puletra. They have completely redecorated the place and have seven large, comfortable guest rooms including one single and six doubles, sharing baths.

Most of the rooms face the ocean, and are done in Colonial style with braided rugs and the like. Each room has been given a name, such as the Americana, in red, white and blue, with pineapple beds; the Autumn Room, in fall colors and furnished in maple; and the York Room, which has a fireplace and velvet fireside chairs. There is also a one-bedroom cottage, once an old railroad station, with private bath and screened porch. House guests are served wake-up coffee each morning (included in the rates) in the Gathering Room or on the porch.

41 Freeman Street, P.O. Box 838, York Beach, ME 03910; (207) 363-4826. (Take Rte. 1A to Short Sands Beach and center of town; bear right at stop sign. Go about 100 yards on 1A; Freeman Street is the first right. Jo-Mar's Guest House is approximately the tenth house on the right.) Rates are moderate, lower by the week. Children are welcome; no pets, please. Open mid-May-Labor Day, and by chance or by reservation from Labor Day-mid-October.

The Bennetts. Robert and Irene Bennett are the proprietors of this beachfront guest house in York Beach. The house offers seven clean, comfortable twin or double rooms for travelers; three bathrooms are shared, two with shower. Guests are welcome to use the living room and glassed-in and screened front porch. There's a piano in the living room for sing-a-longs, and a color TV. A well-equipped kitchen is also available for guests at no charge—to cook a meal or make coffee or tea. The house is nicely located overlooking York Beach's Short Sands area, close to shops and restaurants. Nubble Light House is only a mile away, and the Bennetts say that many of their guests take day trips from the house to Old Orchard, Kennebunk and Ogunquit.

3 Broadway, York Beach, ME 03910; (207) 363-5302. (At the junction of Rte. 1A and Broadway at Short Sands.) Rates are inexpensive. No pets, please; children are welcome. Open May 15-October 15.

OGUNQUIT

One of my favorite memories of Ogunquit is not of a lazy summer's day on the beach but rather of a nasty night in late September. Heavy winds and drenching, chilly rain—the backlash of a hurricane—made going outside a miserable experience. We, however, sat snug and warm beside a roaring fire, feasting on seafood and wine at Perkins Cove. A British companion, more or less enjoying her first experience at tearing apart a whole boiled lobster, mopped at the butter dripping from her chin. She announced that Maine seafood was excellent, if a bit messy.

"However," she added tartly, "when you come to England,

just don't dare make any adverse comments about *our* weather."

The name Ogunquit means "Beautiful Place by the Sea." It is, especially along the winding roads that lead to the ocean. It's a quiet, peaceful town; the residents try hard to keep it that way. The beach is fabulous—clean white sand that goes on and on for three miles. Maine's coast is so rocky that a beach of this magnitude is rare. Usually there are tidal pools, too, where children and adults both can paddle in shallow, warm salt water.

Meandering along the craggy cliffs between Ogunquit Beach and Perkins Cove is the Marginal Way. It is a winding path about a mile long, bordered by blueberry and bayberry bushes, storm-twisted, stunted trees, and bittersweet vines. Benches have been placed here and there along the walk so you can sit, meditate, and admire the perpetually changing sea. Below are coves with masses of gray rocks; if you like solitude these tiny coves are perfect for sunbathing—when the tide is out. A sneaky incoming tide can quickly fill them up, and unless you can scale a cliff very rapidly, you might be taking an unexpected swim.

Perkins Cove at the other end of the Marginal Way is a picturesque little harbor stuffed with boats, both pleasure and working. Shops offering a broad range of things to look at or buy have taken over the once busy fishing shacks on the narrow peninsula alongside. There are several good places to eat, including a couple that specialize in steamed clams and lobsters, served indoors or out. Up behind the Cove, beautiful old houses look benignly down over the hillsides of green lawns or brilliantly blooming gardens.

Shopping—for antiques, clothes, gifts or whatever, is virtually impossible to resist throughout the Ogunquit area. Inviting boutiques and artists' galleries are everywhere. Excellent restaurants, loads of them, offer a variety of cuisines. For more scenic glimpses of ocean and rockbound coast, follow along Shore Drive past Bald Head Cliff. And for a summer evening's diversion, reserve tickets for the current production at the Ogunquit Playhouse. The theater has been presenting top plays with name actors each year since the early 1930s.

Hayes Guest House. Near Perkins Cove on Shore Road you'll find the Hayes Guest House, built around 1830. It's a lovely old New England home, tastefully decorated with Mrs. Elinor Hayes' own collection of antiques. Handmade braided and hooked rugs add their appealing hominess, and every bed is covered with a handsome patchwork quilt. All rooms (five in the guest house with private or semi-private baths, plus two apartments) are air-conditioned and have TV. Coffee is available all day, compliments of the house. Nearby are several good restaurants and lots of shops.

133 Shore Road, Ogunquit, ME 03907; (207) 646-2277. Rates are moderate. No pets, please. Open mid-April-mid-October.

Blue Shutters. Ron and Jean Dahler welcome visitors to their "very special guest house with a personal touch." Blue Shutters is located at the edge of Ogunquit Village on a side street; a little path on the property joins the Marginal Way. It is an old house with gracious Colonial rooms all with an ocean view; each has a private bath. Two of the five bedrooms have a fireplace, and guests may relax in the comfortable living room with TV. A complimentary breakfast is served at your door—whatever time you wish to awake: something home-made, juice, and a carafe of coffee or tea. An outdoor gas cooker and picnic table are available, as is a guest refrigerator. Blue Shutters also offers six fully-equipped efficiency units. All face the beach and are air-conditioned and electrically heated.

6 Beachmere Place, Ogunquit, ME, 03907; (207) 646-2163. Rates are moderate, lower off season. No children or pets, please. Open all year.

Clipper Ship Guest House and Antiques. Guests are welcome in the not one but two handsome old sea captains' houses which make up the "Clipper Ship." Both were built around 1850. One is of Federal architecture, completely modernized but keeping intact all of its old-fashioned charm. There is a lounge with stereo and library, and a comfortable veranda. The other house is large and rambling, with spacious grounds. Both have been furnished by proprietors Kaye and Lois Siegel in a pleasant combination of antique and contemporary. A total of twenty-six guest rooms are available, with either private or shared baths, and there are three efficiencies with private baths.

46 N. Main St. (Rte. 1), Ogunquit, ME 03907; (207) 646-9735. (Located just north of center of town.) Rates are moderate, lower off season. Visa and MasterCard accepted. Open all year.

Hartwell House. Jim and Trisha Hartwell are the owners of this attractive guest house, formerly called The One Sixteen House. During the off season, Jim's parents, Mr. and Mrs. Harold Hartwell, are also around to help welcome visitors. Recently renovated, Hartwell House now offers seven guest rooms and two apartments, all with private baths. An elegant blend of old and new, the house is of contemporary design with skylights, French doors, stained glass and greenery, furnished in Early American antiques. Guests are invited to enjoy the glassed-in, air-conditioned lounge. There's a large back yard, too—over an acre of land—with lovely gardens, grass, and lots of privacy.
116 Shore Road, Ogunquit, ME 03907; (207) 646-7210. Rates range from moderate to expensive, lower off season. Visa, MasterCard and American Express accepted. Open April 15-October 31.

Admiral's Loft. More than 150 years old, the Victorian Admiral's Loft was once a sea captain's home. Today, Frank Sullivan and Bill Wall are your hosts. The house is large, with porches and pleasant grounds, and has ten rooms for guests. Most of the rooms have recently been redecorated with a "country look." Seven share bathrooms, three have private baths. In season (July to September) a continental breakfast is included in the rates. The Admiral's Loft also offers two new efficiency units with air conditioning and color TV.
Main Street, P.O. Box 2232, Ogunquit, ME 03907; (207) 646-5496. (Rte. 1, three blocks north of the village.) Rates are moderate, lower off season. Visa and MasterCard are accepted. No children under 12; no pets, please. Open May 1-Columbus Day.

THE KENNEBUNK REGION

Antique hunters adore Rte. 1. An amazing number of barns, garages, stables and houses advertise old things for sale. Not everyone is charmed, however, by the motley assortment of other establishments scattered haphazardly along the way—overnight cabins and motels, flea and souvenir markets, eating places and what-have-you. Nor is the driver especially thrilled with the condition of some stretches of the road's surface. On my last visit I developed the heart-sinking conviction that something was seriously wrong with my car. Yours, of course, may have better shocks than mine.

An alternate route, taking you almost to Bath, is the Maine Turnpike (I-95). It's certainly faster and is pleasantly lined by nothing but trees. It has another good point: just before reaching the turnoff for the Kennebunk region you will pass underneath a road with a most intriguing name ... Cat Mousam. According to knowledgeable folk at the Brick Store Museum in Kennebunk, there's a story connected with this road, which may or may not be true. Seems there was once a saw mill on the Mousam River. One day a cat chasing a mouse caught—and lost—his tail in one of the saws. The mill thereafter became the Cat Mill, the road, the Cat Mousam.

Exit 3 will take you east to the Kennebunks. They consist of Kennebunk itself, on the west bank of the Kennebunk River, Kennebunkport and Arundel on the east, and Kennebunk Beach, Cape Porpoise and Goose Rocks Beach nearby. It's all one great big summer colony and has been ever since the Civil War. Even the Indians liked it, regularly setting up summer encampments along the shore. The beaches are long and broad, fine for swimming or lazing in the sun. Fishing is excellent, both surf and deep sea. Kids, and most likely their parents, may enjoy taking an old-time trolley ride at the Seashore Trolley Museum in Arundel.

Kennebunk was, long ago, a shipbuilding town. On Rte. 9A/35 you will pass a raft of splendiferous mansions built by shipyard owners and sea captains. They're all frilled and gussied up in true Victorian style; the most outstanding of all is the famous Wedding Cake House.

Kenneth Roberts, the late author of many New England historical novels, lived in Kennebunkport. Dock Square, just beyond the river, teems with specialty shops and galleries. Ocean Avenue, leading out of the Square, takes you past some magnificent scenery, including Spouting Rock and Blowing Cave. Throughout Kennebunkport—in town, along the shore drive, or out in the country—you can admire countless more examples of New England's gorgeous big old houses. You may even stay overnight in some of them!

1802 Guest House. Although it's just a short walk or bike ride from the village, the 1802 House offers a delightfully peaceful country atmosphere. In winter, cross-country ski trails start right at the doorstep. In the summertime there is excellent golfing nearby, and swimming or sunning at the easily accessible beaches. Bob and Charlotte Houle and family have owned the 1802 House since 1975, and have redone the interior in Colonial style including charming period wallpaper and natural woodwork. The handsome pine staircase in the front hallway was constructed long ago by a local sea captain. There are eight guest rooms, plus two efficiencies. Two of the rooms are extra large and have a fireplace. Most have private baths; two are semi-private. Guests are invited to enjoy the comfortable lounge/game room. Outside are grills, lawn chairs, umbrella-topped tables and a sundeck for guests' use. The Houles offer a full breakfast at a reasonable extra charge, served in the cheerful dining room. Bag lunches for beach or travel are also available upon request, and in the off season a luncheon of homemade chowder, sandwiches and dessert is served. The coffee pot is on year-round.

Locke Street, P.O. Box 774, Kennebunkport, ME 04046; (207) 967-5632. (Turn left just beyond Dock Square at the white Chamber of Commerce sign and follow North Street. The sign for 1802 House is on the lefthand side, first left after St. Martha's Church. If you're coming by bus or plane, the Houles will provide transportation to and from airport or bus terminal upon advance notice, for a slight charge.) Rates are moderate, lower off season. Efficiencies are available from June to September, by the week only. Visa and MasterCard are accepted. Well-behaved children are welcome; no pets, please. Open all year.

The Chetwynd House. Captain Seavey of Kennebunkport built this house around 1840; in later years it was owned by artist Abbott Graves, known for his scenes of Kennebunkport social life in the early 1900s. (His work is on view at the Brick Store Museum in Kennebunk.) Today, the blue-shuttered house is owned by Susan Knowles Chetwynd. Mrs. Chetwynd, a perfectly delightful lady, has earned a well-deserved reputation for serving her guests fabulous breakfasts, included in the rates. A few of her unusual specialties are boned chicken in cheese sauce, baked haddock, mushrooms on toast, and oyster stew. There's always fresh fruit, too, beautifully presented—such as melon filled with strawberries or blueberries. Visitors come to Chetwynd House from all over the world, and the breakfast table is a favorite place to meet and share experiences over the delicious food. Guests may also have coffee, tea or cocoa during the day, and on rainy afternoons there might be a full tea with little sandwiches and cakes.

Mrs. Chetwynd has five guest rooms; one has a private bath, the others share two baths. All are cheerful and very comfortable, furnished with antiques and period pieces. The Gable room (with its own bath) includes a handsome cannonball bed and blue velvet chairs. Touches of blue, Mrs. C's favorite color, may be seen all through the house, which is graced with long windows and the original wide, pine floorboards. The pleasant living room/library offers a whole wall of well-filled bookshelves for guests' enjoyment. Outside is a lovely little garden; even though all the activity of the village is only steps away, a feeling of seclusion and peacefulness pervades.

Chestnut Street off Ocean Avenue, P.O. Box 130, Kennebunkport, ME 04046; (207) 967-2235. (From Dock Square take a right on Ocean Avenue and go two blocks.) Rates are moderate to expensive. Open all year.

The Captain Lord Mansion. A very special place indeed, the Captain Lord Mansion is a bit more expensive than most guest houses. But if you've ever wondered what it would be like to spend a day or so in a house listed on the National Register of Historic Places, here's your chance.

Nathaniel Lord (just between us historians) was not actually a Captain. He was a merchant and shipbuilder, a prominent citizen of Kennebunkport. In 1812, the British blockaded the harbor, and Lord's shipwrights had little to do. To keep the men occupied, he had them build the most magnificent mansion in town. The Federalist-style house includes 25 rooms, twelve fireplaces and a museum's worth of other splendid touches.

Some of the light fixtures are of real silver; the bathrooms have marble sinks and clawfoot tubs. There is a graceful four-story spiral staircase, a three-story suspended elliptical staircase, and an octagonal cupola (with widow's walk) on the roof. Floors are the old, wide "pumpkin pine." All of the 15 guest rooms (including five very large suites) are done in individual styles and are completely furnished with antiques, some with the original pieces. The rooms range in size from 17' x 17' to 22' x 22', and 10 have working fireplaces which guests are invited to *use*. One room even has its own private little elevator. Windowseats, handmade quilts, braided rugs and live plants all add to the charm of this remarkable house. There is also a ghost.

Her portrait hangs over the fireplace in the music room (which has the original French wallpaper). Her name was Sally Buckland; she was the daughter of Charles P. Clark, President of the New York/New Haven Railroad and grandson of

Nathaniel Lord. There is also a photograph of Sally's wedding in 1898, when she was 24. She loved the house with a passion and wanted all of its glories preserved forever. Her grandchildren recall being frequently admonished not to step on the rugs or damage any of the furniture. Since her death there have been a number of spooky incidents, so it is said—footsteps, lights mysteriously going on and off. The obvious explanation is that Grandmother Buckland stalks the house, checking to see that all is well. To be on the safe side, please be sure and wipe your feet when you enter.

Rick Litchfield and Bev Davis, proprietors, will happily show you more—and there's lots more—of the architectural marvels of the elegant mansion. And as not just the soul needs sustenance, they include breakfast, with homemade muffins, hot breads and soft-boiled eggs, in the rates. Breakfast is served at a big, long table in the kitchen next to a huge wood stove. Guests are also invited to use the sitting room with its working fireplace and many books, and the game room, well-supplied with games of all kinds.

Special four-day "Weekender" affairs are held annually. One celebrates Halloween, with a cheese and wine party, pumpkin carving, and a costume party. The Christmas Weekender takes place over the three weekends preceding the holiday. Guests gather for a wine party and carol sing, make old-fashioned tree decorations, and—accompanied by a blazing fire and warming spirits (alcoholic, not spectral)—trim a real Christmas tree.

P.O. Box 527, Kennebunkport, ME 04046; (207) 967-3141. (Take Exit 3 from Maine Turnpike; take left on Rte. 35 and follow signs through Kennebunk to Kennebunkport. Bear left at traffic light at Sunoco station; go over drawbridge and take first right onto Ocean Avenue. Then take fourth left after Texaco. The mansion is on the second block on left. Park behind building and follow brick walk to office.) Rates are expensive. No children under 12; no pets, please. Open all year.

The Captain Jefferds Inn. This handsome structure, a recent addition to Kennebunkport's fine collection of guest houses, vies in elegance with the Captain Lord Mansion across the street. White clapboard with black shutters, the house is of Federal design (with later 19th-century additions) built in 1804 by William Jefferds, Jr. Warren Fitzsimmons and Don Kelly are your cordial hosts. Antique dealers and designers (a former residence and the Inn have both been featured on the covers

27

Guest Houses

The Captain Jefferds Inn, Kennebunkport, Maine

of *House Beautiful*), they have decorated the mansion with unusual American antiques. Included are brass beds, handmade quilts, wicker and rattan, folk art and special collections such as majolica, tramp art, and the like. And nothing is behind glass! In the adjoining antiques barn, guests may browse and/or purchase collectibles.

There are eleven guest bedrooms in the main house: one single, seven doubles and three triples. Five have private baths, three are semi-private. Some offer fireplaces and harbor views; most have designer Laura Ashley wallcoverings, and each room has been done in a different mood. The "Belle Watling" room, for example, is reminiscent of *Gone With the Wind*. Fresh-cut flowers add to each room's charm. In addition, three apartments in the barn (all with private bath) may be rented either as separate bedrooms or as efficiencies by the day, week, month or season.

Guests are encouraged to enjoy the public rooms as they wish. The large living room, with fireplace, is decorated with colorful chintz-type fabrics, the walls a warm misty yellow. A comfortable sun porch is filled with plants and looks out to the harbor, and there's a TV and game room, too. Outdoors is a spacious lawn for sitting and sunning; attractive wicker furniture (for which the owners are well known) is arranged in pleasant conversational settings.

A generous country breakfast featuring homebaked breads or muffins and fruit in season is included in the rates, served either in the gracious formal dining room or in the Pine Room around an old trestle table. Your hosts also serve afternoon tea, beside a crackling fire if the weather allows. The house is only a few minutes away from Dock Square with its many shops, galleries and restaurants. Beaches, boating, fishing, golf and tennis are easily accessible, as are tours of historic houses. Messrs. Fitzsimmons and Kelly will be delighted to make arrangements for any activity you desire, and plan special trips. *Pearl Street, Box 691, Kennebunkport, ME 04046; (207) 967-2311. (Follow Ocean Avenue 3/10ths of a mile; at Arundel Wharf go left to Pearl Street.) Rates range from moderate to expensive, lower off season. Children over seven years are welcome. No pets, please; your hosts have four dogs and an equal number of cats. (Many guests, according to the owners, vie with one another as to which animal will share their room with them!) Open all year.*

Country Gardens Inn. Mrs. Harry E. Jordan's lovely old home on Kennebunkport's Ocean Avenue is surrounded by greenery and flowers. The house is about 100 years old, and Mrs. Jordan has lived there for 25 years. Guest bedrooms include one single and four double or twin, sharing two baths. In addition, there is a two-room suite for two or three people with three twin beds and private bath. Guests are invited to share the large, attractive living room, furnished with antiques. And there is a pleasantly shaded open porch with plenty of chairs for summertime relaxing. Mrs. Jordan offers tea and snacks, and for an extra fee also provides breakfast, served from 8:30-11:30 a.m. There is a restaurant next door, or guests may walk to Dock Square, half a mile away.
Ocean Avenue, Kennebunkport, ME 04046; (207) 967-2050. Rates are moderate. No small children, please. Open June 15-October 15.

The Green Heron. Named for the herons which occasionally come to the river to feed, this guest house has a sort of barefoot, hot-summer's day informality. Virginia and Wallace E. Reid have been running the Heron since 1965; they once owned and operated a whole group of local inns. Built around 1908, the house originally provided food and lodging for the staffs (coachmen, footmen, etc.) of wealthy summer residents. Today there are ten guest rooms, all with private baths, plus a separate housekeeping cottage. A full breakfast served in sunny rooms overlooking the water is included in the rates, and prepared by Mrs. Reid, renowned locally for her good cookery. Outdoors, guests may sit on the porch or relax on lawn chairs overlooking the river.

Ocean Avenue, Kennebunkport, ME 04046; (207) 967-3315. (Near the mouth of the Kennebunk River, one mile from the village.) Rates are moderate. Visa and MasterCard are accepted, if absolutely necessary. Open June 1-mid-October.

**English Meadows Inn,
Kennebunkport, Maine**

English Meadows Inn. Helene and Gene Kelly, and their daughter Claudia, thoroughly enjoy showing guests around their comfortable old Victorian home just outside of Kennebunkport. Buttons, a lovable lump of a sort-of-sheepdog, will be there, too, to greet you at the door. The house is situated on seven acres of meadow, with fruit trees and pine groves, flower gardens, and forty or more hundred-year-old lilac trees. Come, if you can, when the lilacs are in bloom . . . the scent is downright breathtaking! And deer sometimes come to graze in the pines and meadows in the early morning.

The main house holds twelve guest rooms, with brass and iron beds; several more rooms are currently being added. There are eight semi-private baths; each room has running water. Braided or hooked rugs cover the wide pineboard floors; old prints, handmade quilts and coverlets, hanging plants and fresh flowers add further welcoming notes. In addition, the attached Carriage House offers more accommodations with paneling, a large central room with stone fireplace, and early wicker furniture. Here, say the warm and friendly Kellys, is where "the young folks" like to stay. A complete breakfast, included in the rates, is served in the main house's cozy old kitchen accompanied by lots of good conversation.

Located only a mile from the ocean and a half-mile walk to town, the "Meadows" has the nice feeling of being way out in the country. Bicycling is a great way to explore the area—bring your own or the Kellys will tell you where you may rent one. Kennebunkport and Kennebunk offer a wealth of delightful shops and galleries, excellent restaurants, and public golf courses. There's fine swimming at Kennebunk Beach, and deep sea fishing is easily accessible. Antique enthusiasts don't even have to leave the grounds: the Kellys operate their own shop at English Meadows—Whaler Antiques—where you'll find country furniture and accessories, quilts, hooked rugs, baskets, wicker, folk art and unusual collectibles.

RFD 1, Rte. 35, Lower Village, Kennebunkport, ME 04046; (207) 967-5766. (From the Maine Turnpike take Exit 3 to Kennebunk; turn left on Rte. 35 south and go five miles—English Meadows will be on your right.) Rates are moderate to expensive, lower off season. No children under 12, please. Open April 1-November 15.

OLD ORCHARD BEACH/PORTLAND AREA

Moving on along the coast, a jog eastward will take you out to Old Orchard Beach. A seven-mile, exceptionally wide crescent beach is the big draw here. It's very busy indeed in summer, the beach and large amusement pier attracting thousands of visitors. Small cottages and hotels of varying sizes extend all along the shore road. Quaint it is not, but if you have children with you they might enjoy a stop-over for swimming and spun sugar.

Portland, twelve miles away, is Maine's largest city. Walking tours (you can pick up maps) take you through several historic areas and past lots of stately mansions of Federal, Greek Revival and Italianate architecture. Early in its history, Portland was often attacked by Indians, and the British bombarded and burned it in 1775. In the 1800s the largest commercial sailing fleet on the Eastern Seaboard operated out of the harbor. Fire destroyed much of the city in 1866, but its citizens quickly rebuilt. The Old Port Exchange, a restored waterfront area, is great fun to explore. Note the handsome hand-carved signs hanging outside its shops. Portland offers an impressive array of excellent restaurants, too, many of these located in The Old Port Exchange.

Another point of interest is Portland Head Light out near Cape Elizabeth. One of the oldest lighthouses in the country, it was erected on the orders of George Washington and beamed out its first warning beacon in 1791. A somewhat different attraction not far away is L.L. Bean's famed emporium of outdoor apparel and gear. To get there, drive 18 miles northeast from Portland to Freeport on Rte. 1. Bean's is open 24 hours a day, 365 days a year.

Sea-Ward on the Ocean Front. A large, comfortable beach house, gray-shingled Sea-Ward was built in 1915 as a family summer home. It was extensively remodeled to serve as a guest house, and is now owned and operated by the second generation of the original owners. The nine spacious bedrooms are tastefully decorated; all but one room has its own bathroom with shower. There is a large living room with fireplace, and both a sun porch and screened porch, each with a sweeping view of the ocean. Each morning complimentary coffee, tea and cocoa are served around the fireplace. The beach is just outside the door, with wonderfully clean, fine sand and no undertow—the tide goes out 500 feet from high to low tide. "Perfect for sand castles!" according to Mrs. Nelson B. Record, proprietor. She adds that they put on outdoor roasts on the beach from time to time, and when strawberries are in season they hold strawberry shortcake parties. (Guests share the cost.) Sea-Ward is located in Pine Point, a small lobster fishing village, part of Scarborough. Old Orchard is only a couple of miles away, Portland ten miles. Nearby are excellent seafood restaurants, public tennis courts, and scenic drives galore.
Bliss Street, Pine Point, Scarborough, ME 04074; (207) 883-6666. (Three miles from junction of Rtes. 1 and 9 at Dunstan Corner in West Scarborough. Going north on the Maine Turnpike take Saco Exit 5, South Portland Exit 7 going south. Continue toward Old Orchard Beach—Pine Point is 2½ miles north.) Rates are moderate, lower off season. Visa accepted, if absolutely necessary. No dogs, please. Open May 15-October 15.

Huston Tourist Home. George and Amie Huston's guest house is in Westbrook, five miles northwest of Portland. It's a beautiful old three-story house built around 1881. The Hustons have two twin bedrooms, one with an extra couch which can be used as a bed, two rooms with wash basins, one large room with a sun porch which can sleep five (a family), and one small single. In addition, there are three rooms on the third floor which are sometimes available for two persons each on weekends or if not otherwise occupied, during the week. Bathrooms are shared. There are many restaurants close by, and you can easily drive into Portland for dining and sightseeing.

741 Main St., Westbrook, ME 04092; (207) 854-2325. (Rte. 25, five miles from Portland, three miles from Exit 8 on the Maine Turnpike.) Rates are inexpensive. Open all year.

BATH/WISCASSET/BOOTHBAY HARBOR/ DAMARISCOTTA

The old seaport of Bath, on the Kennebec River, has been a shipbuilding center for more than 200 years. And the Bath Iron Works, which began building ships in the late 1800s, still launches new vessels regularly. Be sure and pay a visit to the fascinating Maine Maritime Museum, located at four separate sites. During the summer months you can take a boat cruise along the river from one display to another, including a shipyard where wooden sailing vessels are still being built. Washington Street, lined with magnificent 18th-century mansions, is another Bath attraction not to be missed.

From Bath, follow Rte. 1 to Wiscasset, ten miles north. Wiscasset claims to be Maine's prettiest village, and may well be. It comes as a surprise—you crest a hill and there it is. Picturesque Main Street, with its brick sidewalks and handsome old homes, begins at the curve. The road then slants sharply downward, ending abruptly at the broad Sheepscot River. Just to the right of the bridge, you'll see two derelict sailing ships, the four-masted schooners *Luther Little* and *Hesper.* Photographers seem to like them, and they *are* old. I find them depressing. But Wiscasset is not, and the hilly little town of Wiscasset offers a number of interesting things to see. The Old Jail and Jailer's House are fun to explore, and the Nichels-Sortwell Mansion, an 1807 sea captain's home, offers a grand display of period furnishings. There's also a fine selection of antique and craft shops.

The Boothbay Region lies east of Rte. 1. Here the coast of Maine goes berserk, shooting out narrow needles of land into the Atlantic. Although the region encompasses several vacation communities, the hub of activity centers mainly around Boothbay Harbor, reached by following Rte. 27 east just across the bridge after Wiscasset. Boothbay Harbor is studded with boutiques and restaurants, delightful to explore. Several types of boat excursions leave from here, too. The *Balmy Days* will take you to Monhegan, furthest out in the bay's chain of islands. The *Argo* offers shorter cruises around some of the other islands, and a chance to see lobstermen at work, seals, and with luck, a rare bird like the osprey. In early July an impressive parade of old sailing vessels takes place, along with other events, during Windjammer Days.

From Boothbay Harbor, head back to Rte. 1. The twin villages of Newcastle and Damariscotta, separated by the Damariscotta River, are only a few miles further on. The Chapman-Hall House in Damariscotta, built in 1754, is fun to tour; the old kitchen (the original) is particularly interesting. All of the peninsulas along this stretch of coast are worth seeing, but my favorite destination is Pemaquid Point, reached from Damariscotta via Rtes. 129 and 130. You can return to Rte. 1 via Rte. 32, which will bring you out again just before Waldoboro, a bit north.

At Pemaquid Point, rugged cliffs overlook descending shelves of granite. Wild roses and spicy balsam scent the air in summer. One of the nicest ways of spending an hour or so on a hot day is to stand braced between two ledges, bare feet in the swirling water, absorbing the coolness—or to be more accurate, the iciness. Seagulls wheel and scream raucously overhead, sometimes engaging in furious battle over a bit of bread tossed by a picnicker. It's possible, too, to spy a seal basking on the rocks or showing a sleek black head above the water. Inside the abandoned lighthouse building on the cliff is a small museum with some interesting nautical photographs and artifacts, including a rare, preserved blue lobster.

Grane's Fairhaven Inn. This exceptionally attractive guest house, situated in peaceful country surroundings not far from Bath, has a lengthy history. The original house was built in 1790 by Pembleton Edgecomb for his bride, and the Edgecomb family occupied the house for 125 years. In 1926, the house was purchased by the Gillies, who named it Fairhaven. They added more rooms on the west side in the 1940s, but the east facade was left virtually unchanged. The George Millers took ownership in 1969 and for almost a decade worked at restoring and refurbishing the place. In 1978, Jane Wyllie and Gretchen Williams bought Fairhaven and have been welcoming guests to their pleasant country home ever since.

Your cordial hostesses have nine guest bedrooms including one single, six doubles and two queens, sharing four nicely-appointed baths. The rooms are large and very comfortable, some furnished with antiques and all with homemade quilts. Those in the front have a splendid view of the Kennebec River; 300 feet of the inn's property edge the water. Rooms at the rear look out on a sloping, wooded, granite-rocked hillside. For guests' enjoyment there are the Tavern, a BYOB bar with a fireplace and piano, and the comfortable Library with a large collection of books, color TV, stereo and another fireplace. Outdoors the flagstoned patio or tree-edged lawn are delightful places to sit, contemplate the view, and soak up the country silence.

Activities galore are available throughout the year. Grane's Fairhaven is set on 27 acres of lawns, woods and fields—for sunning, hiking, picnicking, cross-country skiing and snowshoeing. Reid State Park not far away offers a fine beach for swimming, and has picnic facilities. Golfing, boating and fishing are easily accessible, as are duck and deer hunting in the fall. The nearby towns of Bath, Brunswick, Wiscasset and Boothbay Harbor provide a wealth of shops, galleries and restaurants. (You'll need a car.) For entertainment there are the Performing Arts Center in Bath and the Music Theater in Brunswick.

A generous country breakfast is provided at a small extra charge, served in the charming dining room. Homemade muffins and breads are specialties, along with delicious jams and jellies (also homemade). Depending on the day, guests are also offered juices, fruits in season such as melon or bananas in French cream, eggs, hash browns, pancakes (perhaps blueberry or apple-cinnamon) or orange French toast, hot or cold cereals, souffles of cheese or ham, omelets, mixed grills, Scotch eggs, scrapple, eggs Benedict or Finnan Haddie! Plus plenty of excellent coffee, tea or hot chocolate. In winter, dinner is also available, upon advance notice. And your hostesses thoughtfully provide menus from restaurants in the area, for browsing through.

No. Bath Road, Bath, ME 04530; (207) 443-4391. (From Rte. 1 north of Brunswick—before reaching Bath—take New Meadows exit and follow signs about three miles west to Grane's Fairhaven. Look sharp for the last sign; it's at a sudden left turn just past the golf course.) Rates are moderate; reduced weekly and monthly rates are available. Well-behaved children and pets are welcome. Open all year, except for two weeks in March.

Guest Houses

The Roberts House. Situated right on Wiscasset's Main Street up a few steps from the old red brick sidewalk, this historic structure is now a bed and breakfast establishment. Francis Blyth, a trader, built the house around 1799 for his wife. Her father, Captain Ebenezer Whittier (John Greenleaf Whittier's uncle), provided the land. During the War of 1812, Captain Binney, leader of the regiment at Fort Edgecomb, occupied the house. Later owners included Thomas Cunningham and Charles Knight.

In the early 1970s, a local bank purchased the place—planning to raze it and erect a new bank building on the site. But irate depositors threatened to withdraw their money if such desecration were carried out, and so the handsome old Federal house was sold instead—to Edward and Alice Roberts. They took ownership in 1973; and in 1981, (their two daughters grown up and away at school) the Robertses opened the house to guests. Currently, Roberts House welcomes travelers throughout the summer months. Ed and Alice spend their winters in California, where Ed teaches English in Ventura.

The Roberts House offers three guest bedrooms: one twin, one double and one with double and single beds. Two baths are shared, one with tub and one with shower, and the double room also includes a sink. A blue and white color scheme predominates in the attractively furnished rooms. Downstairs, there's a pleasant sitting room with lots of comfortable chairs, and a music room with piano and books. Side porches and a small backyard offer more areas where guests may sit and relax.

Alice Roberts offers her guests a full breakfast, included in the rates. There'll be fresh fruit, homemade breads or muffins —perhaps including her specialty, sourdough biscuits—and eggs, coffee, tea or cocoa. Your hostess always provides delicious extras, too, like stuffed mushrooms or tomatoes, or sausage. Native Maine blueberries are also a regular part of the repast. The hearty breakfast is served in the dining room, with its colorful Oriental rug, on English Wedgwood and Royal Worcester china. Mrs. Roberts will be delighted to recommend one of the area's many excellent restaurants for other meals. As the house is located right in the village, most of Wiscasset's shops and sites of interest are within easy walking distance.

Main Street, P.O. Box 413, Wiscasset, ME 04578; (207) 882-5055. (Look for the blue sign out front.) Rates are moderate. Children and pets are negotiable. Parking is available. Open June 1-September.

Welch House. Perched atop McKown Hill in Boothbay Harbor, Linda and Scott Sears' guest house has a fantastic view of harbor and ocean. The main house is early 19th-century, once a sea captain's home. A sun deck and huge porch allow guests to loaf in peaceful quiet, while observing all the activity in the harbor below—and many of the rooms have at least three windows with panoramic sea and island views. The eight rooms in the house are furnished in 19th-century style and guests share four baths. Eight wood-paneled rooms are also available in the more modern Sail Loft, with private baths and TV.
36 McKown St., Boothbay Harbor, ME 04538; (207) 633-3431. Rates are moderate. Open early April-end of October or early November, depending on the weather.

Topside, Boothbay Harbor, Maine

Topside. Another guest house on McKown Hill with an even more expansive view is Topside. Owners Faye and Newell Wilson compare the place to being on a ship—hence its name. Built in the 1800s by Captain Cyrus McKown, it is a large white Colonial with black shutters. The rooms, all with private baths, are beautifully furnished in Colonial and Empire antiques. Each has a refrigerator for guests' use. There's also an added modern motel unit. A comfortable library/lounge in the main house is a pleasant place to read or play games. Outside are broad green lawns, nicely landscaped with flowers and shrubbery—with plenty of deck chairs. Wide porches face the island-studded harbor and the open sea beyond.

McKown Hill, Boothbay Harbor, ME 04538; (207) 633-5404. Rates are moderate to expensive, lower off season. No pets, please. Open May 20-November 20.

Hilltop House. Captain Mitchell Reed built Hilltop, on Boothbay Harbor's McKown Hill, as a two-story building. But ship captains in those days were away at sea for great stretches of time, and this one's wife decided that it would be nice to rent rooms—perhaps so she might have some company. The Captain, next time home, agreed. He took the roof off, and added a third floor for extra space. Mrs. Cora Mahr and her husband are your hosts at Hilltop House nowadays, and offer seven guest rooms—some with private baths and others sharing a bath.

McKown Hill, Boothbay Harbor, ME 04538; (207) 633-2941. Rates are inexpensive to moderqte, lower off season. No pets or small children, please. Open all year.

The Brannon-Bunker Inn. Located about five miles south of Damariscotta, this attractive establishment is an ideal place to stay while you're exploring the Boothbay Region. Owners David and Charlene Bunker say that many guests have compared it to the traditional bed and breakfast houses of England and Ireland. There are six guest rooms—one single and five doubles—plus a two-bedroom efficiency apartment. Two of the rooms and the efficiency, all with private baths, were newly added by the Bunkers and are situated in a separate building on the grounds. The other four rooms are in the old barn, which was moved to this site in the 1920s and attached to the Cape Cod house where the Bunkers now live. At that time the building was a rather notorious dance hall called The Hacienda. After years in disrepair, a later owner turned it into guest rooms to house the overflow from her Newcastle Inn. The furnishings throughout are, as Char Bunker puts it, "antique and semi-antique (early attic), and comfortable—not museum-type." Three of the bedrooms and one bath have views of the Damariscotta River.

Guests are welcome to use the large lounge, called the Publyk Room, with its fieldstone fireplace and TV. There's a dining alcove where continental breakfast (included in the rates) is served family style. Offered are a variety of juices, fruits in season, coffee, tea, milk and strictly homemade muffins and coffeecakes or breads, a different kind daily. A guest kitchen is also available for making tea or coffee (makings for both are provided) or keeping food and beverages cold in the refrigerator. In the evenings, your hosts often have a cocktail hour, providing mixes, ice and sometimes a snack or two. Guests report that they enjoy this as it offers an opportunity to meet other guests and compare notes on where to go, what to see, and where to eat.

Behind the place there is a pond, presided over by White Cloud, the Bunkers' resident goose. She, they say, quickly endears herself to all, despite acting as a built-in alarm clock in the summer. And there's plenty of land for children and pets (well-behaved, please) to run off steam. Golf, tennis, ocean swimming, fishing, boating and canoeing are all available nearby. And last, but by no means least, seals may be observed in the Damariscotta River at low tide.

Rte. 129, Damariscotta, ME 04543; (207) 563-5941. (Take Rte. 1 to Business Rte. 1, Newcastle-Damariscotta, then go south on Rte. 130/129. When they split, about three miles from town, stay on Rte. 129 for another mile and a half.) Rates are moderate. Visa and Master-Card are accepted. Open April-October or November, depending on the weather.

The Newcastle Inn. This large turn-of-the-century New England guest house is beautifully situated on the tidal Damariscotta River, in Newcastle. Your hosts, the Thomases, have 18 single or double guest bedrooms plus one that accommodates three people and one for four. Seven have private baths, the others share four baths. All of the rooms are furnished with antiques and are individually decorated. A pleasant living room with fireplace, a TV room, and a spacious screened porch are available for guests' use. An antique shop in the basement offers items for sale including 18th-, 19th- and early 20th-century furniture, accessories, folk art and selected Victoriana. The grounds are lovely, with flowers, trees and shrubbery. Marine facilities are next door. In the picturesque towns of Newcastle and Damariscotta you'll find interesting shops of all kinds, and several good restaurants. Pemaquid Point is less than a half hour away, as is Boothbay Harbor. The

Thomases serve a continental breakfast to guests in season, included in the rates.

Rte. 1, Newcastle, ME 04553; (207) 563-5685 or 563-8878. (Five miles from Wiscasset.) Rates are inexpensive to moderate, lower off season. Children are welcome; extra charge for pets. Open all year.

ROCKLAND/ROCKPORT/ CAMDEN/SEARSPORT

Rockland, once a prosperous shipbuilding town, is today Maine's foremost lobster-catching port. A four-day Seafood Festival is held here each August, with parades, bands, and—naturally—lobsters to eat. From the Maine State Ferry Terminal you can take a ferry ride out to Islesboro, Vinalhaven and North Haven. Vinalhaven, 16 miles out to sea, is not really a tourist mecca—and therein lies much of its appeal. There are 38 miles of paved roads for bicycling; rental bikes and mopeds are available. Fields and roadsides bloom with wildflowers; other stretches pass through cool fir forests. Abandoned granite quarries are now used as swimming holes by the local kids. And one is never far from the sea. Choose a sheltered cove and let the tide creep in around your ankles. Contemplate the horizon. It's not at all a bad way to while away a summer's afternoon . . . there *is* something magical about an island.

Rockport is the home of Andre the Seal. Andre was found abandoned as a pup by Harry Goodridge of Rockport, who raised the seal to stay wild. But proximity to people appealed to Andre more than life with other seals out in the open sea. Eventually, however, he grew too fond of human company and overturned a few small boats in his efforts to make friends. So, for a period of six years, Andre was relegated in the summertime to a special water pen in Rockport's tiny harbor. Each fall he was flown down to Boston where he spent the winter in the New England Aquarium. And every spring the seal was set free to swim home—all the way from Marblehead, Massachusetts, to Rockport, Maine—a 180-mile journey. On one occasion he was greeted upon his arrival in home port by a boatload of Welcome Wagon ladies with a basket of fish! But in 1979, Mr. Goodridge decided that Andre should be returned to the freedom of the sea year-round. Since then, the seal's conduct has been exemplary. During the summer months, he still makes an appearance most evenings in Rockport Harbor where his lifelong friend puts him through a routine of amusing tricks. Andre, a whole-hearted ham, adores every minute of it.

Camden, eight miles north of Rockport, vies with Wiscasset for the title of Maine's prettiest town. It is a difficult choice to make, and I have no intention of trying! Camden's waterfront is unusually lovely, even for Maine. A mountain stream tumbles headlong down from the rounded hills behind, becoming a full-fledged waterfall as it crashes thunderously into the harbor below. Next to it a grassy park offers a perfect place to sit and observe the scene. When it is in home port, you can see the famous Windjammer fleet, as well as masses of other boats. Good restaurants and a myriad of shops abound on every street. Even the lamp posts are attractive, bedecked with flowers. For a terrific view of Penobscot Bay, drive up 1300-foot Mt. Battie, just northeast of town. The only ski area on the coast is nearby, too—the Camden Snow Bowl.

About twenty miles north of Camden, you'll come to Searsport, a famous old seafaring town on Penobscot Bay. Once a busy shipbuilding center, Searsport is still active in maritime commerce today, shipping out massive quantities of potatoes as well as a host of other Maine products. In the Penobscot Marine Museum, located in six different historic structures, visitors can see marvelous collections of ship models, Oriental and American furnishings, nautical memorabilia, and portraits of almost 300 sea captains, all of whom once lived in Searsport.

The Carriage House Inn. Set well off the road at the end of a long, circular driveway, this stately Victorian mansion was built in 1849 by John McGilvrey, a clipper ship captain. Waldo Peirce, a renowned Maine artist, later owned the place. Now, happily for travelers, the gracious old house welcomes guests for overnight or longer stays.

Present owners Louise and Jack Fernan have seven large, comfortable guest bedrooms including two singles, two doubles, two triples and one double suite with adjoining single. The rooms share three baths. A front sitting room with fireplace and color TV is a pleasant spot for relaxing any time of the year, but in winter it's especially appealing with a cheerful log fire blazing away. It also has a fine view of Penobscot Bay. Another room is used for morning coffee, continental breakfast and afternoon tea, all included in the rates. Outside on the spacious lawn, the Fernans plan to add a gazebo and croquet area. A shop (below Waldo Peirce's old studio in the attached carriage house) holds some antiques plus collectibles and contemporary gifts. Guests receive a courtesy discount.

Acadia National Park is 45 minutes away; skiing is available within 30 miles. In addition to exploring historic Searsport, guests may hike along the ocean shore or in nearby woods, go charter fishing, swimming, or take a schooner voyage. The Fernans will be pleased to offer assistance in planning special outings, and will recommend some good places to eat in the area, too.

The house may, it should be noted, have a ghost! Mrs. Fernan believes that the shade of Captain McGilvrey walks the porch of an evening. She'll tell you more.

East Main Street (Rte. 1), Box 238, Searsport, ME 04974; (207) 548-2289. (Just north of town on left side of Main Street.) Rates are moderate. Visa and MasterCard are accepted. Well-supervised children and pets are welcome. Open all year.

The HomePort Inn, Searsport, Maine

The Home Port Inn. Dr. and Mrs. F. George Johnson own The Home Port, another of Searsport's fine old sea captain's mansions on Penobscot Bay. Built around 1863, the house —set on wooded grounds behind a white picket fence—has been beautifully restored and furnished with antiques and period pieces. There are eight guest rooms, sharing four baths, and guests are welcome to explore and use the entire house. A continental breakfast is served, included in the rates. The Home Port is within walking distance of several good restaurants, and for antique lovers there are no fewer than 34 antique and craft shops within the area.

East Main Street (Rte. 1), Searsport, ME 04974; (207) 548-2259. Rates are moderate, lower off season. MasterCard, Visa and American Express are accepted. Children are welcome; pets must stay in kennels. Open all year.

ACADIA NATIONAL PARK/BAR HARBOR

Maine folk don't ordinarily take to superlatives, but even they would probably describe Acadia National Park as "finest-kind." The startling beauty of Maine's seacoast is so concentrated here that it almost hurts the senses. It's not a gentle beauty, the meeting of mountains, forest and sea—it is awesome, and unforgettable.

From the peak of 1530-foot Cadillac Mountain, highest point on the east coast, early risers can be the first in the United States to greet the morning sun. The park extends over some 50 square miles, including about half of Mt. Desert Island. (Although it is a true island, separated from the mainland, Mt. Desert is reached by a short bridge via Rte. 3 off Rte. 1 at Ellsworth.) Follow Ocean Drive and Loop Road for a 20-mile drive up Mt. Cadillac, out to Great Head—a sheer headland jutting over the Atlantic—and past Thunder Hole where the sea surges in, booming and echoing against the ancient rocks. At the Visitor Center, three miles northwest of Bar Harbor off Rte. 3, you'll find park rangers who give guided walks and cruises. Hikers and horseback riders can roam over 100 miles of woodland trails.

Both the French and English claimed the area at one time or another. England won out after a series of wars lasting from 1689 to 1763. But it was French explorer Samuel Champlain who first saw the island in 1604, and named it "L'Isle des Monts Deserts." "Desert," pronounced with the accent on the second syllable, meant uninhabited and wild, not a sandy chunk of land complete with camels and oases.

Bar Harbor, on the eastern shore of the island, was once a small, sleepy fishing village. In 1844 a visiting artist, captivated by the area, carried back word of its spectacular beauty. Affluent families from Boston and Philadelphia began to journey north in ever-growing numbers to spend their summers. Sprawling hotels were built to house them, and a vast number of mansions almost as opulent as the "cottages" of Newport.

Guest Houses

Extravagant spending was the order of the day; dinner parties for 100 or more were not at all unusual.

The long trek to Bar Harbor was usually accomplished by train. Many, however, preferred the sea route, via gleaming yacht. Two gentlemen with simpler (one might say eccentric) tastes, spent a good part of each summer for years sculling all the way down the coast from Boston. Automobiles were not allowed until 1913, so a fine network of carriage roads (still used today) was built to accommodate buggies, cyclists, hikers and horsemen.

At its peak around the turn of the century, Bar Harbor's solid gold way of life slowly went into decline in later years. The Depression, two World Wars, the imposition of income taxes and lack of servants pretty much put an end to the glorious era of lavish living. The Great Fire of 1947 was the final blow. All of the grand old hotels and seventy of the mansions were destroyed.

The fire also decimated the forests along a great stretch of the coast. The trees have come back—the glittering, leisurely life of the late 1800s has not, and never will. But Bar Harbor and Acadia National Park are now accessible to more people than ever. Different people . . . like us.

Thornhedge. If you have a hankering to experience a little of the gracious elegance of Bar Harbor in the good old days, Alonzo and Elinor Geel's Thornhedge can provide it. Until the Geels purchased the house a few years ago it had always been a private summer mansion. It is a three-story yellow and white Colonial built around 1900 by Lewis A. Roberts, a retired Boston publisher. Many of the original furnishings are still in evidence—Chinese tables and a gilt 1810 Phoenix mirror in the foyer, for example. The dining room, where morning coffee, juice and muffins are served free to guests, boasts leaded windows and mahogany period furniture including Chippendale chairs. The salon has a lovely satinwood tilt-top table, a Hepplewhite kettle bench and a pair of Hepplewhite chairs with their original exquisite coverings. Most of the eleven bedrooms, four with fireplaces, have period pieces, too. On the broad veranda one can relax outdoors in the early wicker chairs.

47 Mt. Desert Sreet, Bar Harbor, ME 04609; (207) 288-5398. Rates are moderate to expensive, lower off season. MasterCard and Visa are accepted. No pets, please. Open March 15–November 15.

Mira Monte Inn, Bar Harbor, Maine

Mira Monte Inn. Only a few blocks from downtown, this comfortable guest house (formerly called Sign of the Gull) is set amidst spacious grounds and gardens. It is of Georgian architecture, built before 1880, with wide porches and a rear terrace, four working fireplaces and a handsome open staircase. Your hostess, Marian Burns, is in the process of restoring the grounds to the former Victorian gardens where guests may picnic and play badminton, croquet and horseshoes. She is also redecorating the house in period style, with antiques and reproductions. Ask her to tell you about Bar Harbor's fascinating early history; she is a native of the town and very knowledgeable. Mira Monte has ten guest rooms, eight with private baths, two sharing a bath. Guests are invited to use the library, with a piano, and the living room. Refrigerators are available for keeping soft drinks or fruit, and guests may make coffee or tea at any time. Morning coffee and homemade muffins or hot breads are provided, included in the rates.
69 Mt. Desert Street (Rte. 3), Bar Harbor, ME 04609; (207) 288-4263. Rates are moderate. MasterCard (and possibly others) are accepted. No pets, please. Open May 22–November 1.

Dow Cottage Inn. Another of Bar Harbor's old summer residences, Dow Cottage was built about 150 years ago by hand, with its timber hewed out by a broadax. It is so well-constructed that even today the floors don't squeak! There are eight guest rooms, sharing six baths. Mrs. Ethel R. Black, proprietress, says that Dow Cottage is "just a white, clean house and I try to keep it that way, for lots of guests come back each year. It is no rowdy-dowdy place!" Morning coffee and tea are available for a small extra fee.

227 Main Street, Bar Harbor, ME 04609; (207) 288-3112. Rates are inexpensive. American Express is accepted. No pets, please; children are welcome. Open all year.

Manor House, Inn, Bar Harbor, Maine

The Manor House Inn. Colonel James Foster, a veteran of the Civil War and a builder, constructed this 22-room Victorian mansion back in 1887. It's now listed in the National Register of Historic Sites. Frank and Jan Matter, present-day owners, invite visitors to Bar Harbor to share the manor's gracious ambiance with them. There are eight double guest bedrooms and two two-bedroom suites, all with private baths; two of the rooms have fireplaces. Guests will also enjoy using the spacious public rooms—a main entry hall and a sitting room, each with a fireplace boasting a fine Victorian mantel. A continental breakfast (included in the rates) features fresh fruit and blueberry muffins in season and is served in the sitting room. Two one-bedroom, fully-equipped cottages on the expansive grounds are also available for rental. The Manor House is situated in a quiet residential area within easy walking distance of the village center with its many restaurants and shops. The municipal pier, for cruises and sailing, is at the foot of the street, and Acadia National Park is only minutes away.

In addition, you're entitled to guest privileges, for a small fee, at the Bar Harbor Club located on the water right across the street. The club offers an Olympic-sized pool, five clay tennis courts, spectacular views of Frenchman's Bay, a luncheon room and a bar.

106 West Street, Bar Harbor, ME 04609; (207) 288-3759. Rates are expensive, lower off season. MasterCard and Visa are accepted. Children over 12 are welcome; no pets, please. Parking is available at the house. Open May 15–October 15.

The Ledgelawn Inn. John Brigham, a wealthy shoe manufacturer from Boston, built Ledgelawn in 1904. The Brigham family repaired to their Victorian "summer cottage" each year for the months of July and August. In those days the grounds, far more extensive (60 acres) than they are now, included stables, a barn and carriage house, a gardener's cottage, greenhouses and a gatehouse. All were destroyed in the great fire of 1947, but Ledgelawn survived—one of the very few of the grand mansions that did. The estate changed hands several times over the years and was eventually turned into an inn. Michael Miles, the present owner, purchased the pláce in 1978 and began to restore it to its original elegance.

Today Ledgelawn has 20 double rooms for guests and four with two double beds and two cots; many have working fireplaces. All but four of the rooms have private baths; the others share two bathrooms, a tub and a shower. Most of the furniture and paintings are from the original house or of antique vintage. The honeymoon suite, for example, is furnished with authentic 18th-century French Provincial pieces from another summer estate. A widow's walk that may be used for sunbathing offers a view of a number of mountains, including Mt. Cadillac. And, in addition to all of its other splendid attributes, Ledgelawn has not *one* but *several* ghosts on the premises! Two have been documented by the Society of Psychic Research of New Hampshire and Massachusetts. If you'd like to hear more about them, just ask Mr. Miles.

A bar called the Palm Cafe is a pleasant place to gather and socialize, as is Ledgelawn's spacious—and very beautiful—living room. Breakfast is served, buffet style, in the breakfast room: juice, coffee, imported teas and hot chocolate, eggs Benedict with homemade Hollandaise sauce, crepes or scrambled eggs. And muffins, too! There is a pool on the grounds for guests' use, and guest privileges at the Bar Harbor

Club are available for a reasonable fee. Ledgelawn is within walking distance of many of Bar Harbor's restaurants and shops.

66 Mt. Desert Street, Bar Harbor, ME 04609; (207) 288-4596. Rates are moderate to expensive, lower off season. Visa, MasterCard and American Express are accepted. Children and well-mannered pets are welcome. Open all year.

The Elmhurst Inn. Tall elms and other leafy trees shade the green lawns and large front porch; a driveway leads to plentiful parking in the rear. Furnished with lots of antiques, Elmhurst Inn, an attractive big old house located on a quiet side street, is owned by John Filliettaz. Your hostess is Barbara A. Thomas. There are five rooms with private baths, three semi-private, and two kitchenette units. No food is served, but there are restaurants not far away.

40 Holland Avenue, Bar Harbor, ME 04609; (207) 288-3044. Rates are inexpensive to moderate. No pets, please. Open June 1–October 15.

RANGELEY LAKES/STRATTON/KINGFIELD

Over in the western part of Maine where no lobsters grow are mountains, forests and a multitude of ice-cold lakes. There are around 111 ponds and lakes of various sizes in the Rangeley region alone. The names of the six lakes which make up the Rangeley chain are tongue-twisting evidence that the area was once home of the Abenaki Indians. Besides Rangeley Lake itself, the others are Mooselookmeguntic, Umbagog, Mollechunkamunk, Welekennebacook and Cupsuptic.

It's a stunningly beautiful region, once popular only in summers. Nowadays fall foliage tours, hunting, skiing and snowmobiling have opened it up year-round. The slopes of Saddleback Mountain are the nearest to Rangeley for skiers (7 miles). Sugarloaf/USA, Maine's largest ski resort, is 35 miles away, near Stratton and 15 miles north of Kingfield on Rte. 27. From Kingfield, you can drive 50 miles all the way to the Canadian border over one of the most scenic roads anywhere; just follow Rte. 27 to Coburn Gore. The road travels past rivers and lakes, through wilderness forests and over mountains ... from Eustis Ridge along the way, one can see as far as Mt. Washington in New Hampshire.

Viola's Guest House. Viola herself (Mrs. Viola Kuntz) will perk up your morning (in summers only) with a stack of her own delicious blueberry pancakes! A continental breakfast is included in the rates, but if you want the pancakes—or a light lunch—there will be an extra charge. Mrs. Kuntz donates some of the money to a variety of charities. Her establishment is an attractive old house with brown wooden shingles and white trim, and a porch. It's located on a quiet side street in Rangeley Village, five minutes from the center of town. There are four guest rooms, one with double bed, two with twin beds, and one with double and bunk beds, for families. Everyone shares a bath. There are a few mild restrictions: no drinking or eating in the rooms and only one bath daily. Recently, Viola opened a gift shop on the premises offering her own handmade items such as velvet pillows, fringed tablecloths, booties and macrame.

Pleasant Street, Rangeley, ME 04970; (207) 864-5989. Rates are inexpensive. Open all year. Mrs. Kuntz will, by the way, rent the entire house (which sleeps ten comfortably) for the ski season (December 15–April 15), complete with maid service.

The Widow's Walk. When snow lies heavy on the ground, this guest house in Stratton is a cheerful haven for skiers. But it's also a great place to visit during the rest of the year. The late Victorian house, built around 1892 by the town's leading resident, is gloriously turreted and multi-dormered. (It's listed on the National Register of Historic Places.) There are six guest rooms, all with twin beds and semi-private baths. Mary and Jerry Hopson, assisted by the four other Hopsons, provide friendly, informal hospitality. Breakfast and dinner are included in the rates during ski season; meals at other times may be arranged by advance reservation. Downhill skiing is great at Sugarloaf, only ten minutes away, and the beautiful Carrabassett Valley Touring Center offers superb cross-country skiing with 60 miles of trails. Spring, summer and fall activities include hiking, fishing, canoeing and foliage trips.

Main Street, Box 150, Stratton, ME 04982; (207) 246-6901. (North end of Stratton, on Rte. 27, at intersection of Rangeley Rd., Rte. 16.) Rates are inexpensive, lower from spring to fall. Sugarloaf Credit Card accepted. Open all year.

Guest Houses

The Country Cupboard Guest House. Sharon and Bud Jordan cordially welcome families to their 100-year-old New England farmhouse, on the west branch of the Carrabassett River. They took over the place in 1975 and have renovated and updated it. Mrs. Jordan says that she insists on everything being clean and shiny, with nice amenities like thick towels, heavy blankets, floral sheets and carpeting. Single, double and bunk-bed rooms are available, accommodating 17 people in all, sharing two baths. In summer there is an above-ground pool for swimming, and a screen-house, and loads of places in the area to picnic, hike or fish. In winter guests can snowmobile or cross-country ski right from the door; groomed ski-touring trails are 1½ miles away, connected to 25 miles of more trails. Food is not included in the rates, but homecooked meals are prepared in the kitchen daily for guests who want them. Two historic eating places are within walking distance. The Country Cupboard is only 45 minutes from the Canadian border and 1½ hours northwest of Augusta, Maine's capital.

North Main St., Kingfield, ME 04907; (207) 265-2193. (¼-mile north of Kingfield off Rte. 27, just over a small bridge and immediately on the left.) Rates are inexpensive, special rates for ski weekends and holidays (including meals) are available. Visa accepted. No pets, please. Open from mid July–April 15.

WEST FORKS

This is the big woods country of western Maine, where the only sound you'll hear will be the soughing of wind in the pines. Or the slap of a beaver's tail—there are a lot of those. West Forks is northeast of Stratton and Kingfield, but you can't get there from there. Not directly, that is. What you do is drive down Rte. 16 to its intersection with Rte. 201, and then head north. Rte. 201 follows the Kennebec River up as far as West Forks. There the river veers off, but the road will take you to Quebec City, 140 miles away. Moxie Falls, highest waterfall in the northeast, is nearby. You can try a heart-in-the-mouth whitewater raft trip on the Kennebec, passing through a spectacular gorge, or raft and canoe on the Dead River. Four commercial raft companies are located in the vicinity. Swimming, hiking, fishing and golf are also available, plus hunting in season. In the winter, try snowmobiling, cross-country skiing, and snowshoeing.

Crab Apple Acres. Eleanore and Ben Evans' cozy old farm-house in West Forks dates back to the early 1800s. The seven guest rooms, with handmade quilts on the beds, all overlook the Kennebec River. Christian cross doors and a woodburning kitchen range are some of the interesting features to be found inside the house. Outside, the surroundings are typically, delightfully, Maine "country." There's an old-fashioned garden, and plenty of green grass. Beyond are firred, sloping hillsides—and everywhere there is quiet. All the outdoor activities mentioned earlier are easily accessible, and if you'd like to try whitewater rafting, your hosts will arrange a trip for you. Afternoon tea is included in the rates; other meals are available at extra cost. No liquor is served, but please feel free to bring your own.

Rte. 201, West Forks, ME 04985; (207) 663-2218. Rates are inexpensive for lodging with food, and moderate for American plan (with three meals). Open all year.

BETHEL

Still in western Maine but south of the Rangeley Lakes region is the small mountain town of Bethel, near the New Hampshire border. It lies on the banks of the Androscoggin River and is known for its beautiful old houses, many of Greek Revival style. There are two covered bridges nearby (both constructed in the 1800s) for camera enthusiasts. Summer visitors may explore the Andover Earth Station. It was the pioneer site for communications in space via the original "horn" antenna, and is still a station for international satellite communications and control. Gould Academy, one of New England's many fine prep schools, is located in Bethel, too. A 60-mile tour of scenic Evans Notch (part of the White Mountain National Forest) starts in the village, goes west on Rte. 2 to Rte. 113, through the Notch to Fryeburg, then Lovell, and back to Bethel. Three ski areas are nearby: Mt. Abrams, Sunday River, and Evergreen Valley. Skijoring (being pulled on skis by a horse) is offered at Longhorn Stables at Evergreen, in East Stoneham.

The Edwards Homestead. Built in 1906, the Edwards Homestead was the first house in Bethel to be wired for electricity, and it still boasts the original light fixtures. A large gray house with a long front porch, it's located opposite the Post Office on Main Street. Owners Mr. and Mrs. Cecil Conrad have three rooms available for guests; one bath is shared by all. The house is furnished in antiques. Cathedral window quilts, pillows and other handwork are for sale on the premises. *Main Street, Bethel, ME 04217; (207) 824-2505. Rates are inexpensive. No pets, please. Open all year.*

WATERFORD

Waterford, about fifteen miles south of Bethel at the junction of Rte. 35 with Rte. 37, is one of Maine's most enchanting villages. Surrounding it are miles of lovely, rural countryside with a scattering of blue, fir-edged lakes, low mountains and winding roads. The town itself has been designated a National Historic Site, and coming upon it is like rounding a bend and suddenly being transported back 200 or more years. There's a pocket-sized village green, a brook running swiftly under the road, and a small village center. There's also a splendid bed and breakfast guest house!

The Artemus Ward House, Waterford, Maine

The Artemus Ward House. Lynn Baker is the owner of this historic house, of Federal architecture, opened to guests for the first time in the fall of 1980. Charles Farrar Browne, the 19th-century humorist who created the imaginary character of Artemus Ward, grew up in Waterford. His grandfather built the house in 1805, and Browne, born in 1832, spent his childhood years here. After his father's death, the young man was apprenticed to a printer in Lancaster, N.H., but soon ran away to work on small newspapers around Maine. Eventually, Browne moved West where he worked himself up from printer's devil to journalist on the Cleveland *Plain Dealer.* There he invented Artemus Ward, and until his death in England at age 33, (he's buried in South Waterford, Maine), Browne wrote and lectured as his dryly humorous alter ego. Browne/Ward's satirical views of the world can be compared to his friend and contemporary, Mark Twain. In case you're not familiar with his work, the brochure for the Artemus Ward House includes this sample of his writings, taken from *Affairs Around the Village Green:*

> The village from which I write to you is small. It does not contain over forty houses, all told; but they are milk white, with the greenest of blinds, and for the most part are shaded with beautiful elms and willows. To the right of us is a mountain —to the left a lake. The village nestles between. Of course it does. I never read a novel in my life in which the villages didn't nestle. Villages invariably nestle. It is a kind of way they have.

The Artemus Ward House, which is (of course!) white with green trim, offers four spacious, airy rooms for guests, including three doubles and one triple. One has twin beds, one a queen-sized bed, one a double, and the largest includes a double and a single. All of the sunny, comfortable accommodations are tastefully decorated and very appealing. Two have private baths and two connecting rooms share a bath. Ms. Baker plans to add a powder room on the ground floor. Guests are invited to use the informal lounge/sitting room with a wood stove and a more formal living room with fireplace.

Wake-up morning coffee or tea, and a full country breakfast consisting of fruit, pancakes or eggs, and coffee are included in the rates. In the afternoons (except on Tuesdays) tea is offered both to house guests and the public, from 3 to 6 p.m. Both tea and breakfast are served in the charming tea room done in blue and white, with the original delicate stenciling on the walls. Your hostess lived for some years in England, and her tea fare is authentic—crumpets, scones and pastries, everything homemade and sinfully rich including buttery cakes and creamy trifles. In wintertime, Ms. Baker will also cook dinner for her guests, by advance arrangement at the time of booking.

On Sunday evenings, two young gentlemen—Herb Adams,

Guest Houses

a free-lance writer and historian, and Bill Wood, a local actor—
re-create Charles Farrar Browne and Artemus Ward in a
delightful show presented in the old barn on the grounds.
During intermission Ms. Baker serves homemade ice cream
and cake.

The house is situated on five acres of land, with flowers,
woods and fields. A large meadow sweeps down to Keoka Lake
where you can swim from the private sandy beach or go
canoeing or fishing and—in winter—ice skating. Cross-
country skiing starts right at the door of the house; downhill
skiing, golf, horseback riding and tennis are available nearby.
Autumn visitors may walk to the top of Mt. Tir'em and see
colorful fall foliage reflected in five lakes, or go apple picking
and watch cider being pressed. Ms. Baker will gladly suggest
other activities and recommend restaurants in the area for
evening meals. Antique enthusiasts will be pleased to note
that she operates a shop right on the premises!

*Rtes. 35/37, Waterford, ME 04088; (207) 583-4106. (Right in the
village.) Rates are moderate. Open all year except from
Easter–Memorial Day and October 15–November 15.*

New Hampshire

Some people think of New Hampshire and Vermont as sister states, pretty much identical. They're not. Vermont is gentler, more pastoral, and greener. New Hampshire has a different quality. It is rougher-textured; its mountains are higher, many with barren peaks way above the timber line. It is a fiercer state—even its automobile plates carry the stern legend: "Live free or die."

New England's mountains were originally as tall as the Rockies, but the vast white glaciers from the north filed them down. When the glaciers had passed, less soil was left in New Hampshire than in Vermont, more rock was left exposed. New Hampshire is called the Granite State, for good reason. Still, it is heavily forested—over more than three-quarters of the state. The White Mountain National Forest takes up about 684,000 acres, plus some 47,000 acres more across the border in Maine.

New Hampshire's Mount Washington is the highest peak in the northeastern United States, rising 6288 feet above sea level. There are also 182 other mountains over 3000 feet in the state, comprising several different ranges. They are beautiful, these ancient mountains. Snowladen and white in winter, they appear blue in summer. In early spring, budding trees turn their lower slopes to rosy pink, and in autumn they glow in blazing shades of red, copper and gold.

New Hampshire has its share of rolling countryside, with picturesque little white villages, spic-and-span hill farms and stony pastures. There are lakes, too—more than 1300 of them, and even a seacoast. It is small, but it's there, all 18 miles of it, with some excellent beaches. Portsmouth, a handsome old coastal city, lies at the mouth of the Piscataqua River which separates New Hampshire from Maine.

Out beyond, in the cold waters of the Atlantic, are the nine barren Isles of Shoals, with a long history of shipwrecks and mysterious legends. A summer resort for many years, these islands once were home base for a busy fishing industry.

Guest Houses

Samuel de Champlain sailed along New Hampshire's coast in 1605, and discovered the Isles of Shoals. But Martin Pring, an Englishman, had already explored a bit of the Piscataqua River two years earlier. The early settlements were grants from King James I; the area was later joined to the Massachusetts Bay Colony. In 1679 New Hampshire was named a separate royal province, but boundary disputes with Massachusetts continued to 1741. Then New York and New Hampshire argued over possession of Vermont. In 1764 New Hampshire's western boundary was fixed at the Connecticut River; two years later New Hampshire declared its independence, the first colony to adopt its own constitution.

New Hampshire is a year-round state for visitors. The summers offer countless things to do—exploring birch and pine-edged back-country roads, hiking, swimming, riding, boating and fishing. The non-athletic can spend long hours beside a rushing mountain stream sniffing the exhilarating smell of sun-warmed firs and watching fish in the shallows. Natural wonders abound: caves, gorges, notches, waterfalls and rock formations. You can climb the mountains or ride to their tops via tramways, gondolas, or even a cog railway. And you can collect covered bridges.

Covered bridges are a pleasing sight; photographers and artists adore them, as does everyone else. In summer they are a cool haven from which to watch the water below, or do some leisurely fishing. Many bridges look like narrow barns, most likely because their builders were usually local carpenters who were used to that kind of construction. They were covered, and sided, so they would last longer.

New Hampshire still has a fairly large number of these quaint structures. Vermont has more, about one hundred, but the other New England states have very few left. The ones which do remain are staunchly defended and protected against everything but fire and natural disaster.

In winter the many ski resorts swarm with activity, and in the fall New Hampshire's splendid foliage attracts hordes of visitors. Be absolutely sure you have reservations to stay overnight somewhere before you venture into the mountains in autumn. Around Columbus Day when the leaves are giving their best show, there is literally no room at the inn . . . or guest house.

Roads such as the Kancamagus Highway and Rte. 3 through Franconia Notch can become solidly jammed with cars during

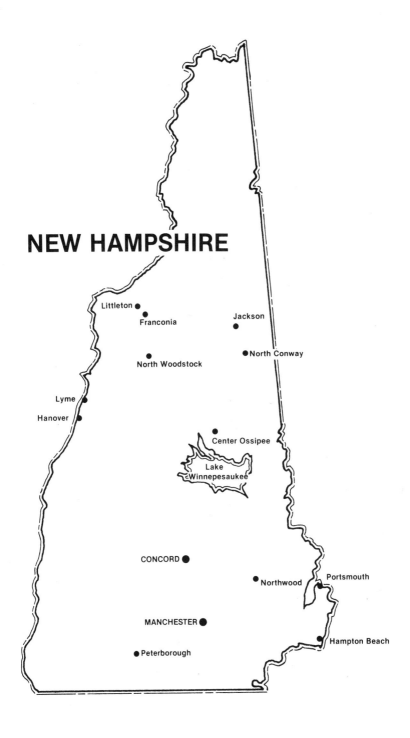

NEW HAMPSHIRE

Littleton ●
Franconia ●
Jackson ●
North Conway ●
North Woodstock ●
Lyme ●
Hanover ●
Center Ossipee ●
Lake
Winnepesaukee
CONCORD ●
Northwood ●
Portsmouth ●
MANCHESTER ●
Peterborough ●
Hampton Beach ●

the height of the foliage season. Be patient—they will move eventually, but a normal 30-minute drive may take several hours. It's not unknown for trapped sightseers to have to spend a night sleeping in their cars. Some smart travelers bring sleeping bags; a night under the stars isn't bad at all, unless it is raining.

Autumn in New Hampshire is a fantastic experience; one can well understand why so many people battle the crowds to see it. The Indians called the annual foliage spectacle "fire on the mountains." And there could not possibly be a more glorious sight than viewing steep hillsides all aflame in a riotous patchwork of colors, while high above the mountain peaks glisten beneath a blanket of early snow.

In election years, and sometimes even the preceding year, February in New Hampshire offers an unusual sport—politician-watching. New Hampshire holds the country's earliest primary, and presidential hopefuls from all over the nation flock to the state. It's a bit like the swallows returning to Capistrano . . . or the buzzards returning to Hinckley, Ohio.

About the only season to avoid in New Hampshire is one that is not ordinarily included in the list—the fifth, or "mud" season. It usually arrives in March, which is not a particularly thrilling month anywhere. One hears dire tales of cars sinking deep into muddy ruts, needing a tow to get out. On the other hand, March and April are maple-sugaring months, in New Hampshire and Vermont both. So if you decide you want to see a sugar house in action, just keep to the main roads as much as possible—and wear boots. You can spot a working sugar shack way off in the distance by its plume of white smoke.

In summer, the weather is warm during the day and cooler at night. Springs are chilly and falls crisp; winters are downright frigid. The cold, however, is drier and far less penetrating in the mountains than it is along the coast.

Sadly, there aren't too many guest houses left in New Hampshire nowadays, although a few new ones have sprung up in recent years. Not every guest house proprietor is interested in publicity, either, and not just in this state. Some do not see any reason why they should advertise. Visitors will come anyway, and if they don't—well, that's all right, too.

I trudged up to the door of one guest house (not to be named) and was met by a rather ferocious older person who most definitely was not interested in providing information. "I ain't got time to faht around with that so't of thing," he grumped, firmly shutting said door in my face. I'm sure he thought I was trying to sell him something. It was rather a pity, too. The house looked quite inviting and was in a nice location on the bank of a river.

I'm certain, however, that even *my* old curmudgeon would prove a better host than he was an interviewee! All the other guest house owners I have met in New Hampshire were friendly, warm-hearted and very hospitable . . . and enormously proud of their ruggedly beautiful, mountainous state.

The major areas of scenic and historic interest in New Hampshire are the White Mountains and Mt. Washington Valley, the lakes region and the seacoast, the Connecticut River region bordering Vermont, and the southwestern Monadnock region. The coastal beaches run along Rte. 1A. I-93 will take you swiftly from the Massachusetts border north to the White Mountains. A jog eastward off I-93, south of the White Mountain National Forest, will get you to Lake Winnepesaukee.

For a splendid circle drive through the mountains, you can take Rte. 3 north through Franconia Notch, Rte. 302 east and south to Conway and the Kancamagus Highway (Rte. 112) west and back to Rtes. 3 or I-93.

PORTSMOUTH/HAMPTON BEACH

Portsmouth, on the Piscataqua River, is an attractive city, settled in 1630. Follow the strawberry signs to Strawbery Banke, ten acres of restored 17th- to 19th-century houses and shops. The first settlers discovered masses of wild strawberries here, hence the name. Restoration of the area began in the late 1950s, and is still continuing. It is a delightful marketplace, with brick and stone sidewalks, intriguing galleries and stores offering countless items, including many with a strawberry motif, and good restaurants. Modern-day artisans live in some of the restored houses, and you can watch demonstrations of all kinds of crafts.

In the city itself are more handsome old houses, built by ship captains and merchants, many open to the public. The Jackson House was built around 1664, the John Paul Jones House in 1758. Commander Jones didn't own the house . . . he was a boarder there while he waited for his ship, the *Ranger*, to be constructed at Kittery, across the river in Maine. The Portsmouth Navy Yard is located in Kittery, too. From the wharf off Portsmouth's Market Street you can sail on the *Viking Queen* out to the Isles of Shoals and Star Island.

There are several state parks along New Hampshire's brief seacoast, including one near Hampton Beach, a busy old seaside resort. Hampton Beach is only a few minutes from Portsmouth; it runs along Rte. 1A and the beach is splendidly long, broad and clean. There's lots of free entertainment all summer: band concerts, pageants, sing-a-longs and fireworks. It is somewhat honky-tonk in appearance, but a very lively place, and fun for families.

At Little Boars Head, North Hampton, travelers may visit the Fuller Gardens. A shaded Japanese garden at the rear has flowering shrubs, a pond and tiny waterfall, and an old footbridge. Beautiful roses and other summer flowers bloom all over the garden, once owned by Alvin T. Fuller, once Governor of Massachusetts. To get there, take the first left off Rte. 1A after passing 101-D.

Martin Hill Inn, Portsmouth, New Hampshire

Martin Hill Inn. A true "bed & breakfast" establishment in the British tradition, Alexandra Gebow's delightful guest house is a welcome addition to the Portsmouth scene. It's composed of two period buildings, the Main House and the Annex. New Hampshire Lieutenant Governor Vaughan sold the land to the Martin family in 1710, for fifty pounds. Around

1820, the old barn—set on a knoll known as Martin Hill—was converted into a house (now the Main House). The Annex, circa 1850, adjoins the house at "backyards" and is just around the corner.

There are six rooms for guests: five doubles, including one with queen-size canopy bed, and one single. Three of the rooms are located in the Main House, three in the Annex. All are air-conditioned, have private baths, and are beautifully decorated in period style. The grounds include a wooded area, which obscures the parking lot, and two bricked patios for sunning and relaxing.

Breakfasts, you'll be pleased to know, are very special at Martin Hill. A typical offering might be juice, fresh fruit in season, omelets with herbs and cheese, pork tenderloin marinated in lemon juice and thyme, freshly-baked scones and jam, plus coffee or tea. And the hearty full-course repast, served in an attractive dining room in the Main House, is included in the rates. Martin Hill is a ten- to fifteen-minute walk from Portsmouth's Market Square and Strawbery Banke with their many fine restaurants and shops.

404 Islington Street, Portsmouth, NH 03801; (603) 436-2287. Rates are moderate. MasterCard and Visa are accepted. Pets are welcome if they can stay with the "resident dog" in the fenced-in back yard. Open all year.

Petrie-Clemons Inn. M. Susan Clemons (a descendant of Mark Twain) is your hostess at this comfortable, tastefully decorated bed and breakfast guest house in Portsmouth. Built around 1815, the handsome three-story brick structure has five rooms for guests including four doubles and one triple, sharing two baths. The rooms, and the house, are furnished in period style: the Brass Room offers an exposed brick wall and an impressive brass bed with patchwork quilt, and the Blue Room boasts a fine mahogany four-poster bed. Breakfast at the Petrie-Clemons establishment is served in the common room, and includes juice, eggs any style, French toast and sausage, and coffee—for a small extra fee. The house is located in downtown Portsmouth, within walking distance of Strawbery Banke and the harbor.

3 Sheafe Street, Portsmouth, NH 03801; (603) 436-4526. (At corner of Sheafe and Penhollow Streets, across from police station.) Rates are moderate. No pets, please. Open all year, but from January 1–April 30 rooms are available only by the week.

Guest Houses

The Inn at Christian Shore, Portsmouth, New Hampshire

The Inn at Christian Shore. Another excellent bed and breakfast establishment in Portsmouth, The Inn at Christian Shore is of Federal architecture, a fine old house built between 1790 and 1800. Its present owners, Louis G. Sochia, Thomas Towey and Charles Litchfield—proprietors of a Portsmouth antique shop—restored and decorated the place themselves. (They live in very attractive quarters in the basement.) There are five pleasant rooms for guests including one single, two doubles and two with twin beds. The two double rooms have private baths, the others share two baths. All are air-conditioned and have color TV. A large, comfortable sitting room, with fireplace, is available for guests' use. And a hearty New England breakfast, included in the rates, is served in the dining room—which also has a fireplace. In spring, summer and early fall, the grounds are green with shrubs and bright with flowers. Restaurants and shops are within walking distance of the house, and Portsmouth's historic 17-century Jackson House is across the street.

Corner of 335 Maplewood Avenue and 5 Northwest Street, P.O. Box 1474, Portsmouth, NH 03801; (603) 431-6770. (From I-95 take Portsmouth Exit 5 to Portsmouth Rotary and go north on Rte. 1 a short distance to Lum's; take Portsmouth Business District exit; at top of ramp bear right onto Maplewood Avenue.) Rates are moderate. Visa and MasterCard are accepted. Children and pets are welcome. Parking is available at the house. Open all year.

The Grayhurst. Peter and Judy Chaput are the new owners of the Grayhurst, located in Hampton Beach, and they have spruced it up with fresh paint, new bedspreads and rugs, and hardwood floors. The rambling, comfortable beach house has 13 rooms for guests, sharing baths, plus several fully-furnished apartments with private baths. There is also a separate cottage with cooking facilities, private porch and accommodations for five people. The large rooms, with full-size double and single beds, have hot and cold water; most have TV. Guests are welcome to use the living room/lounge, and the fenced-in patio in the rear of the house with barbecue grills, picnic table and clothesline (for wet bathing suits). No food is served, but the Grayhurst is only a minute's walk from restaurants, plus all activities.

11 F Street, Hampton Beach, NH 03842; (603) 926-2584. Rates are inexpensive to moderate. Open mid-May through September.

The Century House. The oldest building at Hampton Beach, Century House is a gracious old place, now owned by Allen Morgan. General Ulysses S. Grant once stayed here; his name is on the guest register. (Reading guest registers, by the way, can be very entertaining. Not only are the remarks fun to read, but visitors to New England come from all over the world.) Guests may have rooms in the house, or in the newly-added motel unit alongside; all have private baths. There is a heated pool and a pleasant picnic area with barbecue units. Free morning coffee is included; guests are offered a full breakfast, for an extra charge. The house, which is located at Boars Head, is within easy walking distance of all Hampton Beach activities, shops and restaurants.

522 Ocean Boulevard, Hampton Beach, NH 03842; (603) 926-2931. Rates are moderate, lower off season. MasterCard, Visa and American Express are accepted. No pets, please. Open all year.

THE CONCORD AREA

Concord, settled in 1727, is the capital of New Hampshire. In back of the capitol building the New Hampshire Historical Society has an excellent museum which includes one of the famous Concord Coaches. The State House, built between 1816-1819, is the oldest state capitol in America in which the legislature still meets in its original chambers.

Eleven miles north, in East Canterbury off Rte. 106, travelers may visit Shaker Village, founded by that interesting religious sect in the 18th century. The Shakers, who originated in England in 1747, practiced communal living and celibacy. Their name came from their custom of dancing during religious ceremonies, using a shaking movement. Shaker furniture, now avidly collected by museums, is renowned for its beauty and graceful simplicity. Only nine elderly Shaker Sisters survive today, three in Canterbury, and the rest at Sabbathday Lake in Maine.

South of Concord is the industrial city of Manchester, where the immense brick sprawl of the Amoskeag Mills stretches along the banks of the Merrimack River. At their peak in the 19th century, most of the mills manufactured cotton textiles; the old canals and workers' houses may still be seen. Nowadays, the mill buildings are used by a large number of small manufacturing firms. You can acquire some terrific bargains in this area—for instance, sweaters and other woolens at the Pandora factory store, and shoes at several excellent outlets.

Lake Shore Farm. About half an hour east of Concord, Lake Shore Farm is a great place to stay, especially for families. It is owned by Ellis and Eloise Ring, and was started as a guest house by Mrs. Ring's mother, Lena Watson, in 1926. The 150-acre farm is on the eastern shore of Jenness Pond, in a lovely rural setting. The first house to be built on the grounds was erected in 1848, but Eloise Ring's great-great-great-grandparents settled in the area even earlier, in 1789.

Back in the 1920s when guests were first invited to come and stay, the farm was open only in the summer. Since 1962, however, the Rings have been welcoming visitors year-round. Many come to stay for a week or longer.

There is a large recreation hall with a fireplace, for games and relaxation, and—in the annex—another big living area with fireplace, game tables and a lounge. Tennis courts on the grounds provide a beautiful view of farm and pond. In winter, many snowmobilers come to enjoy the atmosphere and the well-marked trails covering miles and miles of New Hampshire countryside. The spring-fed lake has its own private sandy beach for swimming and sunbathing in summer, and it's well-stocked with fish. Boats and canoes are available for guests' use at no additional charge.

All the guest rooms are light, airy and cheerful. All have a view of the lake, and some even have screened-in balconies.

Lake Shore Farm is really more of a resort than a simple guest house; it's larger, for one thing, and includes meals. There are 30 rooms available in summer and 28 in winter. But it is a charming place, and an excellent choice for travelers who want a base from which to tour the area. (The Rings will supply box lunches for day trips.) And after all, Mother Lena did *start* it as a guest house!

Jenness Pond Road, Northwood, NH 03261; (603) 942-5921. (From Portsmouth, take Rte. 4 west; at Northwood Narrows follow Rte. 107 north; Jenness Pond Road is off 107 to the right. From Concord take Rte. 202/4 east to intersection with 107.) Rates, including three meals per day in summer and two per day in winter, are moderate to expensive. Open all year.

THE LAKES REGION

The lakes of the Lakes Region include Winnepesaukee, Winnisquam and Squam, plus a few smaller ones. Each has its own passionate group of devotees, each has its own distinctive charm and beauty. Scenic country roads curve, climb and dip around the lakes, passing through Colonial villages and famous old resorts dating back to the 1890s. Mountains ring the area; the lakes offer fabulous boating and fishing, with many sandy beaches for swimming.

The largest lake is Winnepesaukee, 28 miles long. The only way to actually see it in its entirety is to climb or drive up a mountain. It is dotted with almost 300 islands, and edged by green forests and innumerable little bays along its approximately 183 miles of ragged shoreline.

Wolfeboro, on the southeastern edge of Winnepesaukee, claims to be the oldest summer resort community in America. It's a peaceful little town with grand old houses and nice shops. The Wolfeboro Railroad takes passengers from the old depot on a two-hour ride to Sanbornville and back. It is a purely delightful ride, accompanied by the nostalgic sound of the train's whistle warning the countryside of its approach. There are some old diesel locomotives, but the best fun is to hop on the steam locomotive-drawn coaches. I prefer the open coaches, although taking along a sweater is advisable. And be prepared to return covered with a fairly thick layer of coal dust. The route passes along a causeway over a small lake, then clackety-clacks its way through woods and fields.

At one point, highway traffic is held up to allow the train to cross. The passengers can't help but feel smug, watching lines of backed-up cars impatiently idling while this smoke-belching, whistle-tooting remnant of the past goes by.

Take Rte. 109 north from Wolfeboro for a splendidly scenic drive; the road swoops down past little inlets where you can see marvelous views of the lake and mountains. Seven miles beyond Melvin Village, turn right on Rte. 171 and go three miles to the entrance for the Castle in the Clouds, in Moultonboro. The mansion was built in 1910 high on a promontory, part of a 6000-acre estate with a panoramic view of Lake Winnepesaukee. You can tour the house, which is fascinating, and go horseback riding over miles of old carriage roads and trails. The road up to the Castle is noteworthy, too; stop along the way and follow the trail to two spectacular waterfalls.

On the other side of the lake, the excursion ship *Mount Washington* leaves Weirs Beach on 3¼-hour cruises. It also stops at Wolfeboro to pick up passengers, and on alternate days at Center Harbor and Alton Bay. The Weirs at Weirs Beach is a popular recreation area in summer, with a large number of amusements including waterskiing, a water slide and dancing. For winter skiing, try Gunstock, just south of Weirs Beach on Rte. 11A in Gilford.

Squam Lake Science Center is an unusually interesting spot to visit, especially if you have children traveling with you. It is in Holderness, on Rte. 25 at Rte. 113, just a few miles northwest of Lake Winnepesaukee. The Center is situated on 200 acres of ponds, forests and streams, and features educational programs, environmental lectures, demonstrations and tours. You can walk through a 100-year-old steam-powered sawmill, see a real blacksmith at work, or catch a glimpse of the future at the operating solar and wind energy exhibits.

From the east side of Lake Winnepesaukee, a short drive (about 13 miles) from Wolfeboro or Melvin Village will take you over to Center Ossipee. The Mt. Whittier Ski Area is six miles north of town, and Lake Ossipee offers swimming and boating. Center Ossipee also has an old stagecoach inn where travelers will find overnight accommodations.

The Hitching Post Inn. Herb and Roberta Lawson are your genial hosts at The Hitching Post. Built around 1830, the structure has been an inn ever since the days when the route —then a dirt road—was the main artery to the north. The Lawsons describe the place today as "just a friendly old inn," and it is exactly that. Herb Lawson will be delighted to regale

The Hitching Post Inn, Center Ossipee, New Hampshire

you with some of his extensive stock of fascinating tales about The Hitching Post's past and its previous owners, one or two of whom were intriguingly feisty characters. And then there is George the Ghost. A spur-of-the-moment invention (I think) of Herb's creative imagination, George "moans a lot and dislikes noisy people." According to Herb, the ghost reports disturbances to him and tells him to do something about them!

For guests, there are six large bedrooms including doubles, triples and quadruples. The simply decorated accommodations are spanking clean and comfortable, and share two baths—one with tub and shower, the other with a stall shower. More baths are planned for the future.

House guests are provided a continental breakfast of coffee and homemade muffins or the like, included in the rates, or you may order a full breakfast. There may also be a "breakfast surprise," but you'll have to discover that for yourself! The Hitching Post also offers dinner—served in four very attractive small dining rooms, all with fireplaces. The specialty of the house is a fabulous Smorgasbord Buffet, set out in the Sleigh Room with its handsome original Ben Franklin fireplace. In summer the Smorgasbord is available seven nights a week; in winter it's offered on Friday and Saturday nights only. Roberta Lawson creates some memorable desserts, too, including—if you're lucky enough to be there on the right day—a delectable peanut cream pie. (No dinners are served on Tuesdays and Wednesdays in winter, but the Lawsons will cook a meal for house guests on those nights if arrangements are made in advance.)

Old Rte. 16, Center Ossipee, NH 03814; (603) 539-4482. (From Wolfeboro, follow Rte. 109/28 northeast to Wolfeboro Center, then 28 to Rte. 16; go north on 16 to Old Rte. 16 and Center Ossipee. From Melvin Village, take Rte. 109 south to junction with 109A; bear left, and then left again onto Ledge Hill Road; follow road over the mountain to Center Ossipee; bear right on Old Rte. 16 and The Hitching Post is at the corner.) Rates are moderate. MasterCard and Visa are accepted. Children are welcome; no pets, please. Open all year (except when your hosts feel the need of a brief vacation which Roberta Lawson calls their "no-smile break")!

NORTH WOODSTOCK AREA

Plymouth, a few miles south of North Woodstock, is called the gateway to the White Mountains. From just outside the town, if you look straight ahead, you can see Franconia Notch far off in the distance—a narrow cut between the mountains.

You can take I-93 or Rte. 3 heading north; I-93 becomes 3 at Lincoln. Lost River, in Kinsman Notch, is off to the left at North Woodstock, on Rte. 112 West. The river runs through a series of glacial caverns and giant potholes, and got its name from its habit of disappearing under the surface here and there. It finally emerges in a stunning waterfall. Youngsters love to crawl through the gorge; adults may use pathways above the caves if they prefer.

The town of North Woodstock itself is small, but with several good places to eat in the vicinity, and a number of shops.

Rte. 112 also goes east from North Woodstock, as the Kancamagus (accent on the "ma," pronounced "mah") Highway. It comes out at Conway, 34 miles away. In between, the Kancamagus is considered to be one of the most scenic stretches of road in the country. It climbs high on the flank of Kancamagus Mountain, crossing a 3000-foot high pass. All along the way are swift, rocky streams, and there are numerous outlooks where you may stop and photograph the mountains and forests beyond. It is wild and uninhabited country, and travelers in the very early hours of the morning might even see a moose tranquilly grazing beside the river road.

Although New Hampshire has some 1500 bears nowadays, it's not likely that you will ever spot one, even here. If you do, be reassured: according to the state's Fish and Game Department nobody has been known to have been killed by a bear in New Hampshire since the Revolutionary War. Tame bears, another story entirely, may be admired at Clark's Trading Post one mile north of North Woodstock on Rte. 3. In summer, the animals hang around atop platformed posts and wait for travelers to place bear food in small cups which are then hauled up on a pulley—by the bears.

Cascade Lodge. The Lodge, now owned by Tony D'Antuono and Rita Smith, was built around 1890. It is a large white structure, right on North Woodstock's main street, with a 7-foot-wide, 100-foot-long porch—with lots of chairs for sitting. From the porch, guests have a splendid view of mountains and a cascading river across the road. Inside, the house is, as Tony and Rita put it, "old and quaint, including squeaky floors." There are 13 rooms for guests in summer, including three singles, six doubles, two triples and two suitable for four persons; in winter 11 rooms are available. Two baths plus a lavette are shared and, the owners note: "There's never a lack of hot water." Much of the house is furnished in antiques and the rooms are done with wallpaper, not paneling. Guests are welcome to use the large living room with TV and upright piano; the grounds are pleasantly green with shrubs and flowers. No food is served, but there are restaurants within walking distance. Hiking, skiing, scenic drives and camping are all within a 10-mile radius; for a cooling dip in summertime, ask your hosts to tell you about the excellent nearby swimming hole.
Main Street (Rte. 3), P.O. Box 95, North Woodstock, NH 03262; (603) 745-2722. (From I-93 take Exit 32, bear right at the traffic light at end of ramp and then right at next traffic light.) Rates are inexpensive, lower off season. No pets, please. Open all year.

The Maywood. The Maywood, a white Colonial with a long front porch, was built around 1900. The house, which includes some of owner Mrs. Marion Fadden's antiques, has ten rooms for guests, sharing two baths. In addition, there are six cottages, fully-equipped and heated. Cable TV is available both in the cottages and the guest house. Guests are welcome to make use of the living room in the main house, with books, magazines and daily newspapers. In warm weather, you may sit out on the porch or on the large front lawn under nice old shade trees. The Maywood is a two-minute walk from the center of the village, and Mrs. Fadden will be pleased to suggest a good restaurant nearby.

Rte. 112 West, North Woodstock, NH 03262; (603) 745-8363. Rates are moderate. No pets, please. Open late May–mid-October.

FRANCONIA NOTCH/FRANCONIA VILLAGE/ LITTLETON

Beautiful Franconia Notch is an eight-mile pass between the Franconia and Kinsman ranges of the White Mountains. As you enter the Notch from the south, Cannon Mountain is on your left; Liberty, Lincoln and Lafayette Mountains are on the right. Just before the Notch don't miss Indian Head to the left, the rock profile of an Indian and his feathered headdress (of trees). In the Notch itself you will come almost directly to the entrance gate to the Flume, on the right.

The Flume is a deep, narrow gorge carved out by the force of the Pemigewasset River; it extends 800 feet along the flank of 4460-foot Mt. Liberty. Steep granite walls, formed long before the Ice Age, rise 60 to 70 feet on each side, varying from 12 to 20 feet in width.

The icy mountain stream tumbles headlong through the gorge from a lacy waterfall at its top. The Flume is deliciously cool; ferns grow from the ancient boulders and the air smells refreshingly damp and woodsy. At the top, continue on around the path to the Pool and Sentinel Pine Bridge.

The Pool, a deep basin in the river at the foot of another waterfall, has emerald-green water so clear you can see pebbles on the bottom. The Sentinel Pine, which fell in the 1938 hurricane, stood on a cliff 150 feet above the Pool. The tree, a white pine, was 175 feet tall with a girth of 16 feet. The late Tom Bodwell, longtime manager of the Flume Reservation, Lost River and Echo Lake facilities, decided that the fallen pine should be made into a miniature covered bridge—which now spans the river just above the Pool.

Bodwell and several other men counted the tree's rings and discovered that it was almost 300 years old. They cut a 60-foot section of its trunk; a team of horses on the other side of the river pulled it across, using a steel cable. Timbers for the top and sides of the bridge were adz-cut, and only hand-carved pine pins were used to secure it.

Continuing on through the Notch you will see an old road going off to the left, leading to the Basin, a large glacial granite pothole at the foot of a small waterfall. Walk upstream, or down, for good wading spots. Or you can fish, picnic, or follow trails leading back into the woods.

Back on Rte. 3 again keep your eyes open for The Old Man of the Mountains. You'll see him high, high up on the left, 1200 feet above tiny Profile Lake. He is a natural phenomenon formed an estimated 500 million years ago, made up of five separate granite ledges in the shape of a man's profile. You can leave your car in the parking lot and walk back along the path around the lake—the Old Man is an unforgettable sight.

Just before reaching Echo Lake, you will arrive at the base station of the Cannon Mountain Aerial Tramway, at the junction of Rtes. 3 and 18. The first aerial tramway in North America, it was built during the winter of 1937-1938. In 1980, the old cars—each of which carried 27 people—were replaced by new ones carrying 80 passengers. The cars, suspended by cables, take you swiftly up the mountain (weather permitting) to the 4200-foot summit. There you can have coffee or snacks, and relax. Then follow the path around the peak; there are superb views in every direction, including one of Echo Lake far below.

From Rte. 3, take Rte. 18 left and northwest a few miles to Franconia Village. The Gale River burbles along through the middle of this quiet little mountain town. Franconia is a popular resort area year-round, with excellent skiing at Cannon Mountain and Mittersill. For an especially fine view of the White Mountains, drive up Sugar Hill on Rte. 117 out of the village. A few miles to the northwest of Franconia, via Rtes. 18 and 302, you'll find Littleton. One of the larger towns in this relatively unpopulated mountain region, Littleton is the area's commercial center with a good selection of shops and restaurants.

Pinestead Farm Lodge. Situated on a 190-acre working farm four miles from Franconia Village, the Lodge is a large white house beside the road, fronted by a row of pine trees. Built by the Sherburn family in 1852, and welcoming guests since 1899, Pinestead is still owned by Sherburns—Robert Jr. and his wife Kathleen. Their next-door neighbors, the Ecks, manage the Lodge itself while Bob Sherburn runs the farm and Kathy operates her new and thriving quilting business, Pinestead Quilts. The two couples have recently refurbished the Lodge with fresh paint, new wainscoting and wallpaper, and some new beds, at the same time maintaining the country charm and atmosphere of the original farmhouse. The accommodations are simple, but clean and comfortable, with six rooms for guests each offering a double and a single bed. (And Kathy's quilts!) The rooms are in groups of three in separate sections of the house. Each group has its own bath and kitchen-sitting room. The rooms are available singly, or each section may be taken as a private holiday apartment. There is also a cottage adjacent to the farmhouse, containing a bedroom, sitting room, kitchen and bath. Wintertime visitors can enjoy downhill skiing at Cannon Mountain, ten minutes away, or head out right from the farm on some 50 miles of cross-country ski trails. Equipment rentals are available nearby. In warmer seasons guests may hike in the mountains, picnic in the farm's wildflower-filled meadows, fish in the river, watch birds, or play tennis, badminton, shuffleboard or horseshoes. In addition, all of the daily activities of the farm are there for guests to wander around and observe. Bob Sherburn raises cattle, pigs, chickens and goats; fresh cider is pressed in the fall and maple sugaring is carried on in the late winter and early spring. Pinestead Farm is a great place for children, with all those animals to admire and acres of space for roaming. No food is served, but you may cook your own or your hosts will be delighted to direct you to some of the area's excellent restaurants.

Rte. 116, RFD 1, Franconia, NH 03580; (603) 823-8121. (Rte. 116 is just south of Rte. 117, coming from Franconia Village.) Rates are inexpensive, with special rates for children, long visits, mid-week ski-season stays and for the cottage. No pets, please. Open all year.

Cannon Mt. Inn. Also on Rte. 116, a shade closer to Franconia, is another guest house in the valley. A large Colonial farmhouse, Cannon Mt. Inn is the oldest in the area. Owned and operated by Gerald A. Kosch, it is a comfortable place with a broad front porch and lots of chairs for relaxing. There are eight guest rooms sharing six baths, and a cottage that sleeps four to twelve people. Guests are invited to use the living room, with TV. A full-course breakfast is served for a small extra charge. Dinners are available for those who wish them; your host specializes in German-American cuisine, using homegrown vegetables. Outdoors one can explore about 200 acres of mountain countryside. There's a swimming hole on the property. A landing strip for planes, a soaring center, two soccer fields, free ski-touring and trout fishing are available, too.

Rte. 116, Franconia, NH 03580; (603) 823-9574. Rates are inexpensive. Children and pets are welcome. Open all year.

Beal House Inn. Built in 1833, this delightful guest house with its relaxing, old-timey atmosphere was once a farmhouse and barn on the outskirts of town. Since those early days Littleton has grown considerably, and now the house, a handsome white Federal-style structure with green roof and shutters, is only a minute's walk from downtown shops and restaurants. Despite its proximity to the center of town, Beal House is wonderfully quiet and peaceful, set on four acres of lawns and woods.

The Beal family purchased the place in the 1930s; when Mr. Beal died a few years later, Mrs. Beal began taking in guests. She later remarried, and as Mrs. Grady, continued to operate the establishment as a guest house plus adding an antique business. The present owners, Doug and Brenda Clickenger, bought Beal House in 1980. Originally from Florida, they traveled some 10,000 miles throughout New England looking at various properties before settling on this one. Since taking possession they have completely refurbished the house and now offer fourteen very comfortable, tastefully decorated rooms for guests, nine with private baths.

Some of the rooms are located in the main house; others are in "The Annex," an addition connecting the house to the old barn. Furnished with antiques, such as canopy beds and wingback chairs, the rooms also include handmade quilts and period wallpapers. A shop on the premises offers antiques for sale—but visitors will be delighted to discover that many of the marvelous old pieces in the rooms may be purchased as well! Guests are welcome to enjoy the pleasant living room with fireplace, an upstairs sitting room, and a deck overlooking the wooded hillside. A glassed-in front porch with wicker rockers offers a grand view of the mountains.

Breakfast at Beal House is locally renowned, served by the fireplace in an attractive breakfast room on long, candlelit tables set with Blue Willow plates. Brenda Clickenger, attired in a cap and long dress, serves the meal, prepared by husband Doug. His specialties are delectable hot popovers and homemade bread, along with fresh fruit, creamy scrambled eggs (offered in charming, old-fashioned hens on nests), waffles, ham, bacon and sausage. Ordinarily no other meals are served, although dinners may occasionally be arranged for groups. Your hosts, however, thoughtfully provide menus from local restaurants for guests to peruse.

Franconia Notch with its many sites of interest is only a few minutes' drive away, and the Mount Washington Toll Road and Cog Railway are easily accessible. The Clickengers will be happy to give you directions to lakes for swimming, mountain hiking trails, and downhill or cross-country ski areas in the region.

247 West Main Street, Littleton, NH 03561; (603) 444-2661. (Junction of Rtes. 18 and 302, one mile east of Exit 42 off I-93.) Rates are moderate. All major credit cards are accepted. Parking is available at the house. Children are welcome and port-a-cribs are available. No pets, please. Open all year.

MT. WASHINGTON/CRAWFORD NOTCH/ JACKSON/NORTH CONWAY

From Littleton, take Rte. 302 east. Along the way you'll see Mt. Washington rearing up against the sky in the distance. It is a challenge, this giant mountain. And if it is the right season of the year you may want to go all the way up to the top. You can walk up, of course, but unless you are a skilled climber, it's not recommended. For most people, there are two other, easier, ways of getting to the peak: the Cog Railway and the Auto Road. In either case, plan a full day for the venture.

The base station for the Cog Railway is six miles from Fabyan, reached via a marked road off Rte. 302. The Railway, first of its kind in the world, has been running almost continuously since 1869. The cars are pushed by specially-built steam locomotives; their horizontal boilers are tilted lower in front, so that the water level remains even while on the mountain. And they're cute, all spiffily painted in bright colors.

When the train reaches Jacob's Ladder, where the grade is 37.41%, the soot-grimed conductor may come walking through the train, at an odd angle, seemingly. That's the moment to try and stand upright; you will be fighting gravity and it won't be easy. Cameras and binoculars appear to be floating straight out before you. When it is time to descend, the engine *backs* down the mountain, the cars joggling along behind it.

Even on a rainy day the trip is exciting ... the trees alongside become ever smaller, more stunted and bent. Then most of them disappear entirely as the train claws its way above the timberline. Outside the train windows only huge, tumbled boulders can be seen, greenish with lichen. Sometimes there are rare Alpine plants, too. It is a menacing world up there, harsh and primeval, always blasted by ferocious winds. It is also colder at the top, often chillingly so; be sure and bring a jacket or sweater.

Don't let the steepness of the grades or the quaint appearance of the train stop you from making the trip. The Cog Railway is a very safe mode of travel. Not so was the method of descending the mountain used by some local folk in the old days. They simply whizzed down on slide boards, pieces of wood that fitted onto the cograil. The boards were called Devil's Shingles, and a few may be seen on display at the summit. These brave (foolhardy?) souls would climb aboard and let her rip, covering the three-mile descent in two minutes and forty-five seconds. (The train takes over an hour to make the same trip.)

If you would like to try driving up the mountain, the eight-mile Auto Road is on the eastern side. The base station there is off Rte. 16 north of Jackson. The road is a good one, but it's a shade scary for those not used to mountain driving. You might prefer to be driven up in comfort by driver-guides in special van stages. Mobile campers and trucks are not permitted on the road, by the way. And both the Auto Road and Cog Railway are closed in winter.

Mt. Washington has a nasty temperament. The weather at its summit can be unspeakably rotten—such as on April 12, 1934, when the wind velocity was measured at 231 miles per hour, the highest ever recorded in the world. Its average snowfall is 177 inches. And it is cloud-covered more often than not. Washington is not a mountain to be taken lightly; even experienced climbers have met their death on its slopes. Still, ascending it on foot, car or via cog railway is a marvelous experience. The view from the summit is sensational—on a clear day you can see as far as Canada. And even if it is raining or thick with fog, it is a trip worth making.

Rte. 302 south will take you through Crawford Notch, another of New Hampshire's magnificent mountain gaps—one of the most impressive of all. The road curves up and around and down through wondrously wild and awesome scenery, mountains looming thousands of feet above. At the northern end of the Notch, stop and look up at lovely Silver Cascade, a narrow waterfall crashing down a thousand-foot drop.

Crawford Notch State Park is the site of the Samuel Willy House. In 1826 an avalanche crashed down the mountainside. Willy, his family and two hired men heard it coming. Trying to save themselves, they rushed out of the house. The avalanche killed them all—but left the house untouched.

When you reach the town of Glen, turn left (north) on Rte. 16 and then right on 16B through a red covered bridge to Jackson, a charming little town at the southern end of Pinkham Notch. Several of New Hampshire's best ski resorts are in this region: Wildcat, Intervale, Black Mountain and others.

Further on down the Mt. Washington Valley from Jackson is the town of North Conway, noted for its eccentric railway station. It's an irresistible sight, Victorian with a whimsical touch of old Russia. Trains do still run from the station for an hour's ride in antique passenger coaches over 11 miles of track.

Up the street is Carroll Reed's extremely attractive sportswear shop. There are scads of shops of all kinds in this region, and a wealth of places to eat and things to do.

The Village House. Located in tiny Jackson Village, this guest house began as a boardinghouse in the mid-1800s. Called the Hawthorne Inn, it continually attracted guests for more than 100 years. Wintertime visitors began coming in the early 1930s when skiing became popular on a hill in Jackson. The inn became The Village House in the early 1970s. Today Jackie and Ron DeCamp own and operate the place, and offer nine rooms for guests. There are four double rooms with private baths, two with one double and one single bed with private baths, two double with shared bath, and one with two double beds and a private bath. The rooms, decorated with brightly colored wallpapers, are furnished in antiques. Bathrooms are all modern. A large, homey living room with color TV and Franklin stove is available for guests' use, and there is a waxing and storage room for skis in the cellar. Situated on seven acres of land in the center of the village, the house has a splendid view of Mt. Washington, the 18-hole PGA golf course, and the famed Jackson Covered Bridge. On the grounds are a charming gazebo, a pool, and clay tennis courts. A deluxe continental breakfast is included in the rates, and several good restaurants are within walking distance.

Rte. 16A, Jackson Village, NH 03846; (603) 383-6666. Rates are moderate, lower off season, and mid-week winter package plans are available. MasterCard and Visa are accepted. Children are welcome; no pets, please. Open December 15–April 15 and June 15–October 30.

Wildflowers Guest House. Situated approximately 1½ miles north of North Conway village, "Wildflowers" is a charming place to spend a night or two, or more. Ms. Eileen Davies, a most personable young woman, welcomes guests year-round. The house was built in 1879 as a summer "cottage" for James Schouler Esq., designed by the famed Boston architect, Stephen C. Earle. It is white with blue shutters, and has six guest rooms, sharing three baths. Accommodations include some rooms with double and some with single beds. Downstairs, guests are invited to relax around the parlor fireplace or out on the veranda. The wildflower theme is carried out throughout the house, including the cozy, cheerful small dining room with fireplace where Ms. Davies serves a complimentary continental breakfast of coffee, juice, homemade breads, or toast. She will provide a full breakfast too, if you wish, for a small extra charge.

Rte. 16, North Main Street, North Conway, NH 03860; (603) 356-2224. Rates are inexpensive. There is plenty of free parking at the house. Open all year.

Cranmore Mt. Lodge. The oldest section of the lodge, according to owners Bob and Dawn Brauel, is the farmhouse. Built in the mid-1800s, it was converted into a guest house towards the end of the century by the addition of an octagonal wing. At one time, the lodge was owned and operated by Babe Ruth's daughter. The Babe was a frequent visitor, using the house as his hunting and fishing retreat. His former room is now one of the guest living rooms and still sports one of his hunting trophies (a deer's head) and an old barrel table, originally from his trophy room.

There are ten comfortable guest rooms in the main building, called the Inn: four doubles, two triples, three quadruples and one for six persons, sharing four and a half baths (six rooms have sinks). The Inn also offers a cozy sitting room with fireplace, a TV and game room, and an Alpine ski rental shop. In the Barn Loft there are two more rooms, each with two

Guest Houses

Cranmore Mountain Lodge, North Conway, New Hampshire

double beds and private bath, air conditioning, TV and carpeting. There's a modern, carpeted, four-room "Dorm" (designed to accommodate large groups in bunk-style rooms) and a rec room with fireplace. Breakfast, at a small extra charge, is served in the dining room in the Inn. Dinners and barbecues are available for groups, by pre-arrangement.

The grounds at Cranmore Mt. Lodge are lovely, with magnificent pine trees and acres of wooded trails, a mountain stream and even a trout pond (for fly fishing only). A 40-foot pool, an all-weather resilient-surfaced tennis court, a basketball court and a Jacuzzi (hot spa bath) are available for guests' use. Hiking, kayaking, canoeing, bicycling, golf, horseback riding and scenic flights are easily accessible, as are shops, galleries and excellent restaurants. In winter, the lodge offers its own toboggan hill, ice skating pond, weekend snowmobile rides and pizza parties. Five major Alpine ski areas are within minutes, and hundreds of well-maintained trails are nearby for cross-country skiing or snowmobiling.

Kearsarge Road, P.O. Box 1194, North Conway, NH 03860; (603) 356-2044. (Located 1.5 miles from North Conway in the village of Kearsarge. From center of North Conway go two miles north and turn east off Rte. 16 onto Hurricane Mt. Road; proceed one mile and turn south at Lodge sign; Lodge is ¼-mile on the left.) Rates are inexpensive to moderate, lower off season (April 1–June 26 and October 26–December 11). Special midweek and two-night package plans are available. MasterCard and Visa are accepted. Children are welcome; no pets, please. Open all year.

THE MONADNOCK REGION

Mt. Monadnock is the star of this pretty region down in the southwest corner of New Hampshire. The countryside is softer, more rolling, than further north in the White Mountains . . . and there are miles of inviting back roads to explore. A number of covered bridges grace the area, too.

About 60,000 people climb Mt. Monadnock each year on its reasonably easy trails. The mountain isn't all that big—3165 feet—but it does command the entire region. "Monadnock," the local Indians' name for the peak, now is also a geological term for any mountain that stands alone.

In the early 1800s wolves in fairly large numbers lived on the summit of the mountain, dining happily on local farmers' sheep. The outraged farmers eventually dislodged the critters by setting fire to the dead timber where the wolves lurked—reducing the top to bare rock. Monadnock may not be as attractive as when it was tree-covered, but it is wolfless.

Several ski areas are nearby: Crotched and Temple Mountain and Bobcat, among others. The Cathedral of the Pines in Rindge, off Rte. 124, is a summer or fall attraction. It is a nondenominational shrine, and a visit can be a remarkably moving experience. Wooden pews sit on a deep bed of pine needles under a cathedral roof of trees. Beyond the simple stone altar lies Mt. Monadnock; in the fall the view is particularly grand.

Peterborough and Jaffrey are the largest towns in the immediate area, both attractively 19th-century in mood and full of antiques, craft and gift shops and art galleries. In July the Rhododendron State Park in Fitzwilliam (south of Mt. Monadnock) is a gorgeous mass of red, pink and white flowers.

The Willows Inn. A restored historical landmark built in 1830, The Willows is a large white Colonial farmhouse with an attached barn. It sits on a rise above the road, just before the village, and has a picnic table on the front lawn. In the back the ground slopes gently upwards with an apple orchard, pine woods and meadows. Robert Abbott and family now operate The Willows (formerly the Knight Homestead) and have eleven comfortable rooms for guests, some with private baths, others semi-private. A pleasant lobby with TV is available for guests' use, and the Abbotts offer a continental breakfast featuring homemade breads, Danish or coffee rings, included in the rates. Your hosts take a genuine interest in making their guests feel welcome. Ask them for suggestions for things to do in the area; including shops and art galleries, a summer playhouse and concerts, antique shows, hiking and fishing, and —in winter—excellent skiing. Located only a quarter of a mile from the center of Peterborough, The Willows makes an ideal base for exploring the entire Monadnock Region.

Wilton Road (Rte. 101), P.O. Box 527, Peterborough, NH 03458; (603) 924-3746. Rates are moderate. Visa, MasterCard and American Express are accepted. No pets, please. Open all year.

THE CONNECTICUT RIVER/ HANOVER AND LYME

From the Monadnock Region, Rtes. 101, 12 and then 12A will lead you over to the Connecticut River and north. Vermont is just across the river to the west. Directly across from Windsor, Vermont, you'll come to Cornish, New Hampshire and the St. Gaudens National Historic Site. The very beautiful grounds include the home, gardens and studios of the great sculptor, Augustus Saint-Gaudens. On Sundays in the summer months informal outdoor concerts are held in the gardens.

Continue north on Rte. 12A to West Lebanon and then follow Rte. 4 up to Hanover. The home of Dartmouth College, Hanover is a delightful town to explore. Walk around the campus by yourself or take a guided tour—it's an exceptionally attractive college, New Hampshire's oldest educational institution, chartered under a grant from King George III in 1769. Concerts, theatrical events, lectures, art exhibits, and other events go on throughout the year. In early February, Dartmouth holds its famous Winter Carnival, when students compete to create the most unusual ice sculpture.

From Hanover, a winding ten-mile drive north along Rte. 10 will bring you to the small Colonial village of Lyme, and Post Pond.

Loch Lyme Lodge. This pleasant establishment, owned by Paul and Judy Barker, has been taking in guests since 1924. The Lodge, a nice old farmhouse built in 1784, has four guest bedrooms upstairs. One offers a double bed, the others have twin beds, and there is one full bath. Downstairs a large, comfortable living room with a fireplace and piano is available for guests' use, plus another bath. In addition to the Lodge itself,

Loch Lyme Lodge, Lyme, New Hampshire

there are twenty-five cabins dotted about on the extensive grounds.

Loch Lyme overlooks lovely Post Pond, a 40-acre, spring-fed lake surrounded by hills. One hundred acres of woodlands, fields and lakeshore are available for hiking, fishing, cross-country skiing, snowshoeing and sledding. Informal cross-country ski lessons and tours, and equipment rentals, can be arranged with advance notice. For downhill skiers, the Dartmouth Skiway (with two chairlifts and a T-bar) is only four miles away. Loch Lyme had its own waterfront with a beach, boats and canoes. A separate building on the property holds equipment for croquet, badminton and ping-pong, and a small library. There are also two clay tennis courts.

During fall, winter and spring, Judy Barker serves guests a full breakfast, included in the rates. She'll also serve dinner by advance reservation. In summer, from June to Labor Day, Loch Lyme serves three meals daily, but you may choose bed and breakfast only if you wish. Breakfasts are served family style on the sun porch.

Rte. 10, Lyme, NH 03768; (603) 795-2141. (One mile north of town.) Rates for bed and breakfast are inexpensive; special rates for children are available. Cabin rates vary. No pets, please. (The Barkers say that you are welcome to share theirs!) The Lodge is open all year, cabins from late May–mid-September.

Three Church Street, Woodstock, Vermont

Vermont

A trip through Vermont can give you the feeling that you've somehow strayed into the pages of a picture book. Twisty, scenic roads take the traveler through lovely open valleys, stretches of dark forest, and over breathtaking mountain passes, called "gaps." Friendly, crystal-clear streams follow alongside almost every road, appearing first on one side and then on the other. Small, neat villages look exactly like paintings come to life—almost too good to be true. But they are real, down to the last white church steeple and village green . . . the essence of New England.

Vermont is a beautiful state at any season of the year. Springtime is pink and white apple blossoms foaming on the rolling hillsides. Summer is green—green meadows sprinkled with wildflowers, and tree-covered green mountains. Autumn is a brilliant display of gaudily-colored leaves against clear blue skies, and winter is pristine white, all snow and shimmering icicles. No obtrusive billboards mar the view anywhere in the state—they're not allowed.

There really aren't more cows than people in Vermont; it just appears that way. They *used* to outnumber humans, though. In summer, cows seem to be everywhere, grazing placidly in valleys and on rock-strewn upland pastures. They are a peaceful sight, exceedingly soothing, as they munch daisies and eye passers-by with their large, gentle brown eyes. Fewer farms exist today than even twenty years ago, but there are still almost 4000, most of them dairies. They look exactly the way farms ought to, with their photogenic red barns and white houses.

Manufacturing and forestry are other major industries in the state, as are granite and marble quarrying. Vermont has around 100 varieties of marble; some towns even have marble sidewalks. Tourism is very big, too, year-round. Lakes, large and small, offer summer swimming and boating. The fishing is great in both lakes and streams. Hunting for antiques is a popular sport in every season, and the state is full of intriguing shops. Winter ski resorts are many, all excellent. The mountains may not be as high or as rugged as the Rockies or Sierras but the trails provide just as much challenge.

And there is maple sugaring—Vermont is the nation's leading producer of maple syrup, most years. In March and into early April, the traveler is welcome to watch the operators at work collecting buckets from the trees and boiling down the sap over hardwood fires in the sugar shacks. The sugar-makers often hold sugar-on-the-snow parties for visitors. Hot, fresh syrup is poured into a pan full of packed clean snow. The sticky concoction is called a "leather apron" and traditionally is eaten along with doughnuts and sour pickles (the latter to cut the sweetness).

The Green Mountains, part of the Appalachian chain, run all the way down the center of the state; Mount Mansfield is the highest, rising 4393 feet above sea level. Vast chunks of Vermont are wild; 262,000 acres belong to the Green Mountain National Forest. A sturdy hiker can walk the length of the state on the 260-mile Long Trail, which took twenty years to cut.

Beautiful Lake Champlain, 125 miles long, forms the boundary between New York State and northwestern Vermont. Samuel de Champlain was the first to explore the region, in 1609. A number of French and English settlements and forts were established in later years. In the mid- to late-1700s Vermont was claimed by both New York and New Hampshire, causing some hot and heavy arguments.

The settlers who were caught in the middle were not pleased. They were told by New York that they had to pay new fees for every acre they had already purchased. Some of them resisted with force and were arrested as rioters. A militia called the Green Mountain Boys led by Ethan Allen was formed to protect the settlers. That feisty band later carried out the first aggressive act of the American Revolution, in May, 1775. They captured Fort Ticonderoga from the British, virtually waging their own private war.

Vermont then declared itself an independent republic, with its own coinage and postal system, and a clause in its constitution prohibiting slavery. In 1791, Vermont joined the Union, the first state admitted after the original 13 colonies.

The best way to see the state is to choose a route and mosey along, visiting historical sites or other points of interest on the way. Rte. 7 is a good choice, beginning at the northwest border

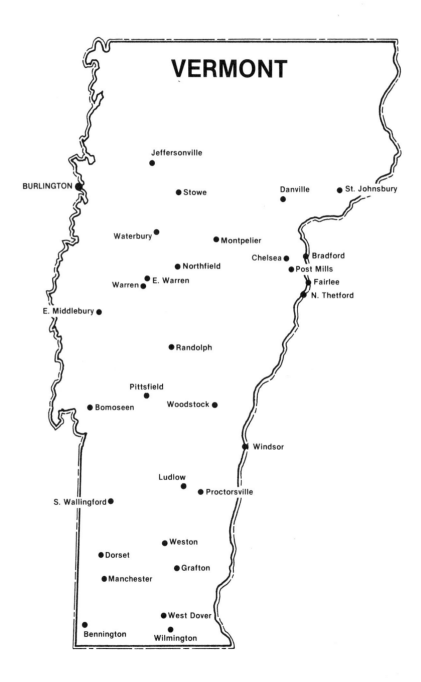

VERMONT

Jeffersonville

BURLINGTON

Stowe

Danville

St. Johnsbury

Waterbury

Montpelier

Chelsea

Bradford

Northfield

Post Mills

Warren ● E. Warren

Fairlee

N. Thetford

E. Middlebury

Randolph

Pittsfield

Bomoseen

Woodstock

Windsor

Ludlow

Proctorsville

S. Wallingford

Weston

Dorset

Grafton

Manchester

West Dover

Bennington

Wilmington

of Massachusetts and heading north along the western side of Vermont all the way to Burlington. From Burlington you can take a side trip northeast to Jeffersonville, Mt. Mansfield and Stowe.

Rte. 100 south from Stowe will bring you to Waterbury, then down through the middle of Vermont, ending up in Wilmington not far from the Massachusetts border. Another scenic road is Rte. 12 south from Montpelier to Woodstock. Or you can take Rte. 2 from Montpelier northeast to St. Johnsbury. From there you may continue on to New Hampshire's White Mountains, or take Rte. 5 south following the Connecticut River along Vermont's eastern border to Norwich and cross over the river into Hanover, New Hampshire.

But don't feel you have to restrict yourself to any one route. Winding side roads are everywhere, leading to other routes or particular areas and towns, so explore with abandon. The only time you will find the roads really heavy with traffic is during the fall foliage season. (That is mispronounced "foilage" by a number of irritating people who ought to know better.)

In autumn, Vermont's dark green firs, white birches and gray outcrops of granite provide perfect foils for the almost unbelievable splashes of crimson, gold, bronze, russet and peach-tinted leaves. The peak of color is usually around Columbus Day, one of our newly moveable holidays. In general, the foliage season lasts from mid-September to mid-October. (Newspapers, radio and television throughout New England will keep you informed daily—sometimes it seems minute-by-minute—of the progress of foliage perfection as it moves slowly southward from Canada to Connecticut. Vermont even has a special 24-hour telephone hot line to call for the latest information!)

Vermont's weather is what you'd expect for a northern mountain state. Summer days are generally pleasantly warm but can get nippy at night. If you plan to go hiking or mountain climbing, take along a sweater; even midday can be cool at higher altitudes. Winters are very long, and very cold, with a great deal of snow most years.

Many Vermont guest houses are open the year-round, to accommodate both summer sightseers and winter skiers. Reservations are imperative during the foliage season, and reassuring to have the rest of the year.

No matter where you go in Vermont, there will be ski resorts nearby. It is, after all, the most mountainous state in the country. Downhill and cross-country skiing are the things to do in Vermont in the winter months, but you don't have to ski to enjoy your visit. You can go snowmobiling or snowshoeing, instead. Another option is to avoid the slopes altogether and prowl between tall snowbanks along the streets of small mountain towns observing the colorful array of ski outfits, or you may simply admire the magnificent scenery. Indoors you'll most likely find a blazing fire, just the place for relaxing with a book or good company.

If you do go in wintertime, please remember to put snow tires on your car. Vermonters are usually well-mannered about pushing or pulling people out of drifts, but it's wise not to test their patience too far.

Sinclair Lewis once described the natives of Vermont as "a complicated, reticent, slyly humorous lot." Calvin Coolidge has often been held up as the perfect example of a typical Vermonter. Their humor *is* very dry, but nowadays most seem to be as loquacious as any other New Englander. And many still speak with the unique, vowel-twisting accent of old Vermont. President Coolidge, it is said, excelled in this. Even other Vermonters were impressed with his pronunciation of "cow"—in four syllables.

Route 7—Bennington to Burlington

BENNINGTON

A graceful 306-foot stone monument commemorates the Battle of Bennington, fought on August 16, 1777. Today the monument offers a grand view of the surrounding area. An elevator takes visitors to the observation platform. The battle actually took place a few miles away in New York State, but this is where the Americans' ammunition was stored.

General John Burgoyne desperately needed the supplies to help his troops cut off New England from the other colonies. He sent an army of 800 Hessians and Indians to capture the storehouse. To the general's astonished disbelief, the rebels, under General John Stark of New Hampshire, soundly trounced the British forces—including later reinforcements. British casualties were 207 killed or wounded, 600 taken prisoner. The Americans lost only 14 men, and 42 were wounded.

Guest Houses

The Battle of Bennington was considered a turning point in the American Revolution. It weakened Burgoyne's command; two months later he and his battered army surrendered at Saratoga.

The oldest Stars and Stripes flag, from the same battle, is on display in the Bennington Museum. The museum has a fine collection of early American glass, Bennington pottery and Grandma Moses paintings. The Grandma Moses Schoolhouse, the same one she attended as a young girl, is on display, too. And the Old First Church, Vermont's Colonial Shrine, is well worth a visit. The poet Robert Frost is buried here in its ancient graveyard.

Mount Anthony Guest House. A white clapboard Victorian, the house is located in downtown Bennington. Henry and Elizabeth DeGrenier are the proprietors. It is comfortably furnished, with eight guest rooms; two have private baths, two are semi-private. Guests enjoy the glassed-in porch, and outdoors the pleasant yard with big trees and a swing.
226 Main Street, Bennington, VT 05201; (802) 447-7396. Rates are inexpensive; weekly rates are available. No pets, please. Parking is available at the house. Open all year.

Colonial Guest House. Charles and Josephine Reis welcome visitors to their 100-year-old restored Colonial home, located two miles from the center of Bennington. There are seven rooms for guests, all pleasantly furnished and immaculately clean. Most rooms share a bath; all but one has its own sink. Some rooms have air conditioning and black and white cable TV. Typically old New England, the handsome house has two parlors with comfortable chairs and love seats, and lots of books and magazines. Food is not included in the rates, but the Reises will be happy to provide an old-fashioned family-style breakfast or dinner if you order in advance. The meals are served in two large dining rooms, one with a fireplace made of bricks from an old schoolhouse. Outdoors you may sit on the patio in the sun or under shady trees and enjoy a panoramic view of the mountains. The house is on a hill, and the Bennington Monument is clearly visible—on another hill, in the distance.
Business Rte. 7 North and Orchard Road, Bennington, VT 05201; (802) 442-2263. (On Harwood Hill.) Rates are inexpensive; weekly rates are available. Open all year except Christmas and Easter.

MANCHESTER & MANCHESTER CENTER

This lovely area, surrounded by mountains, has been drawing summer visitors for more than a century. Now, with some
of Vermont's best skiing nearby, it's a year-round attraction
with tree-shaded streets, several excellent art galleries, and
scads of unusually interesting gift and antique shops. For col-
lectors of miniatures, the Enchanted Doll House in Manchester Center is a special delight; it is an 1812 farmhouse
with many rooms full of games, dollhouses and antique dolls.

Manchester's Southern Vermont Art Center is a popular
place to visit while you're here, too. Film and music festivals
are held every summer at the Center, in a Colonial mansion
with beautiful grounds. And the Equinox Sky Line Drive, five
miles south of Manchester, has spectacular views of southwest
Vermont all the way up to the summit of the mountain—3861
feet. It is a toll road, off Rte. 7, open from May to November.
Sometimes, even in summer, fog or rain may close it down
temporarily.

If you have the urge to zoom down a mountain on an indi-
vidually-controlled sled, you can—on the Alpine Slide at Big
Bromley Ski Area, eight miles east of Manchester on Rte. 11.
A chairlift gets you up the mountain. Then it's all downhill,
nearly a mile of hairpin turns, curves and straightaways. The
Slide is open May to October, weather permitting, and it's fun!

Munson 1811 House. An absolutely elegant house—yet with
a wonderfully homelike atmosphere—this is a black-shuttered
white New England Colonial, set amidst lovely lawns and
huge old trees. One of the oldest structures in Manchester,
the original house is believed to have been erected in the
1770s; the roof, however, was raised in 1811, giving the place
its name. Two brothers, Jerod and Samuel French, held the
original land grant. During the American Revolution Ethan
Allen, of Green Mountain Boys fame, confiscated the land
from the Frenches (who were British sympathizers) and sold it
to a family named Munson. Thaddeus Munson was a captain
in the Continental Army. He, so the present owners say,
haunts the rooms now called the Munson Suite.

In 1903, Mary Lincoln Isham, Abraham Lincoln's grand-
daughter, bought the house. Among other changes, Mrs.
Isham added bathrooms—but almost immediately ordered
the bathtub in her maid's room removed because, the story
goes, she found the sound of the girl splashing in it annoying!

Guest Houses

The Henry Robinson family purchased the place in 1939 just prior to Mrs. Isham's death, and operated it as an inn for four decades. Jeffrey and J. Claire Eade have owned Munson 1811 House since 1980, and have completely restored it, furnishing the rooms with antiques from various periods. In addition, they have turned what was once a private speakeasy run by Mrs. Isham's son into a cozy English pub, complete with fireplace. The Eades have also restored the six acres of grounds to their former splendor, including a magnificent rose garden.

Guests may choose the Jerod French Suite with two double beds and a fireplace; the Munson Suite with four single beds and a fireplace; Martha's Room (Martha was Jerod French's mistress) with two single beds and a fireplace; Luella's Room, or The Hidden Room, each with one double, or Mary Lincoln's Room with two single beds. The decor in each is charming. All have private baths and include an array of nice extra touches such as books and magazines to read, scented soaps, and hard candies to munch. A continental breakfast, consisting of juice, coffee and sweet rolls (included in the rates) is served in the dining room, done in Wedgwood blue. On chilly mornings a fire blazes in the fireplace. Guests are invited to enjoy the formal parlor and large library, too, both with fireplaces.

Main Street (Rte. 7), Manchester, VT 05254; (802) 362-1811. Rates vary from moderate to expensive; weekly rates are available. No small children, please. Open late May-November 1 and December 1-April 1.

Heritage House. Another fine old guest house on Manchester's Main Street, Heritage House is owned and operated by Mrs. Pearl McLear. It is an attractive house of Victorian vintage, filled with antiques. There are five rooms for guests, one with private bath, the others sharing a bath. There is a large living room for guests' use, too. Mrs. McLear does not serve food, but she will be pleased to recommend the best places to eat, and interesting shops to visit, in the area.

Main Street (Rte. 7), Box 605, Manchester, VT 05254; (802) 362-1412. (Opposite the Library). Rates are inexpensive. Well-behaved children and pets are welcome. Open all year.

DORSET

Dorset—a decidedly enchanting mountain town—is just off Rte. 7 on Rte. 30, six miles northwest of Manchester Center. Its sidewalks are marble; the country's first marble quarry was opened nearby in 1785, 17 years after the town was settled. Throughout the area one glimpses through the trees or beside the road, old, abandoned, sheer-walled quarries, the water below a dark jade green. Artists and writers love Dorset; many have settled here permanently.

Maplewoods Farm Guest House. Mr. and Mrs. Leon B. Edgerton own Maplewoods, a 200-year-old Colonial home located a mile north of town. It is a large white frame house wih green shutters. There are seven guest rooms sharing four baths; corner bedrooms have a grand view of the mountains. Guests are welcome to use the spacious family room with TV; in winter there will most likely be a cheerful blaze crackling in the fireplace. In addition, there are an attached greenhouse, a pretty little pond on the spacious grounds, a grove of sugar maples ("sugar bush" it's called up here), and a private airstrip. A fine cross-country ski-touring center is only three miles away, well-maintained and free to all. Breakfast and dinner are available at Maplewoods, for an extra charge.
Rte. 30, Dorset, VT 05251; (802) 867-4470. Rates are moderate. Children and well-trained pets are welcome. Open all year.

The Little Lodge at Dorset. This delightful guest house of-fers just about everything a visitor to Vermont could ask for. The setting is ideal—on a hillside overlooking a trout pond and surrounded by wildflowers, white birch and pine trees, with a mountain beyond. Behind the lodge is a forest laced with trails for strolling, bird watching or cross-country skiing. According to owners Allan and Nancy Norris, the old Colonial house was an antique when it was moved to its present site more than 50 years ago. Several additions have been made to the original structure, each in keeping with its architectural style. The house includes some lovely antiques, fine paneling, foot-wide floorboards and period wallpaper.

There are three double rooms for guests, and one triple. Four bathrooms include two with shower, one with tub and shower and one half bath. Guests are invited to enjoy the barnboard-walled den with TV, fireplace, wet bar, and refrigerator for storing drinks or picnic lunch "fixings." The den also has a dartboard; another room offers a ping-pong table. The living room with wood stove where guests may sit and read quietly is well stocked with books.

Included in the rates are a light breakfast and, occasionally, afternoon tea. Homemade banana bread or coffeecake are breakfast specialties, served on the hexagonal sun porch in warm weather. At cocktail time (BYOB), crackers and Vermont cheese or fondue are offered. Three excellent restaurants are located in the village of Dorset; one is within easy walking distance, the others within a two-minute drive. Many more restaurants, and shops of all kinds, are within a six-mile radius. Ask the Norrises to tell you about them, plus nearby state parks, hiking trails, skiing, fishing, bicycling, tennis and golfing (one course is across the road). For further entertainment, try the Dorset Summer Playhouse.

Rte. 30, Box 673, Dorset, VT 05251; (802) 867-4040. (About one block north of the Village Green.) Rates are moderate. There is a kennel with two indoor-outdoor runs, and quiet, well-behaved dogs are allowed to stay there for a small extra charge. Children are welcome. Open all year.

SOUTH WALLINGFORD/RUTLAND/ BOMOSEEN

Back on Rte. 7 again, heading north, you'll pass through the South Wallingford area, about 14 miles south of Rutland. Here you are close to several ski resorts: Killington, Pico Peak and Round Top. Supposedly, Vermont was named from the top of Mt. Killington. In 1763, a pioneer preacher, Rev. Samuel Peters, rode to Killington's summit. The lush panorama of green spreading out in every direction led him to heights of inspiration ... and he christened the land "Verd-mont" or "green mountains."

That's one version. Another, less picturesque, is that French explorers named the state—*Les Verts Monts.*

Rutland is the home of the Vermont State Fair, held each September, starting on Labor Day and lasting a week. Farm animals, arts and crafts exhibits, maple sugaring and all manner of produce are on display. Just a few miles northwest of Rutland, on Rte. 3 in Proctor, there is an excellent marble exhibit where you can see how marble is quarried and watch a sculptor at work (closed in winter). Proctor also boasts Wilson Castle, a splendid sprawl of architectural magnificence built in the mid-1800s on a 115-acre estate, with a fine collection of European and Oriental furnishings and sculpture.

And over to the west of Rutland, via Rtes. 4 and 30, you'll find Lake Bomoseen, a popular resort area.

Green Mountain Tea Room & Guest House. Built in 1792, this historic house was originally a stagecoach stop and tavern on the old stage road from Bennington to Rutland. Here the driver would exchange his tired horses for fresh ones, and, most likely, have a convivial drink and catch up on local gossip in the tavern. Herb and Peg Barker are your genial hosts nowadays. Five rooms are available for guests; three were once one large room—the upstairs ballroom. Two baths are shared. Guests are welcome to use the large living room with color TV, a piano and books. And afternoon tea is most definitely served! Peg Barker offers 15 varieties of tea in colorful individual pots, along with yummy homemade desserts or Vermont cheese and crackers. Green Mountain is a charming Colonial house at the side of the road in a peaceful rural setting, on eight acres of land bordering Otter Creek. Guests may canoe, fish, picnic and swim right there. Hiking, bicycling and hunting are also popular activities; hunting and fishing licenses are available at Green Mountain. The rates do not include food, but the Barkers serve delicious homecooked meals at reasonable prices—in addition to tea.

Rte. 7, South Wallingford, VT 05773; (802) 446-2611. Rates are inexpensive to moderate. Children are welcome; pets must stay with owners at all times. Open all year.

The Country Bed and Breakfast. Polly and George Dolber welcome guests to their charming old New England farmhouse in Bomoseen. It's nicely located in a peaceful country setting at the end of a quiet road, only 1000 feet from Lake Bomoseen. Guests may roam over several hundred acres of woodland hills and open pastures. Swimming, boating, fishing, golf, horseback riding and antiquing are all available nearby, as are excellent restaurants. (A car is needed.) For skiing, Killington and Pico Peak are only 45 minutes away. There are two rooms for guests, one with double bed and a very large room with twin beds. Both are air-conditioned, and share one bath. Guests may also use the spacious living room with TV, a screened-in porch, and outdoors, the shady lawns. As the name states, a hearty breakfast is included in the rates.

Bomoseen, VT 05732; (802) 273-2023. (From intersection of Rtes. 4 and 30, go north on Rte. 30 4½ miles, then left on dirt road across bridge straight to the house.) Rates are moderate; special weekly rates are available. Children and well-behaved pets are welcome. Open all year.

MIDDLEBURY/BURLINGTON/
LAKE CHAMPLAIN ISLANDS

As you continue north to Burlington on Rte. 7 from Rutland, you will come to Middlebury. The Starr Library at Middlebury College has a fine collection of works by Robert Frost. The Morgan Horse Farm, operated by the University of Vermont, is just off Rte. 7, 2½ miles northwest. It's where the remarkable Morgan horses are bred and trained; about 60 horses can be seen and there are guided tours of the barns and paddocks.

In 1795 a singing-master named Justin Morgan brought a colt from Massachusetts to Randolph, Vermont. That first Morgan—named Justin Morgan after its owner, turned out to be an amazing creature. A distinct new breed of horses descended from him, all sturdy-legged, deep-chested, swift, graceful, courageous and intelligent. That sounds like an awful lot of adjectives for a horse, but the Morgan is all of those and more.

It became America's war horse; General Custer rode a Morgan—and an entire regiment was mounted on Morgans during the Civil War. Mounted police prefer Morgans, and they are also superb trotting horses.

Further on, at Shelburne, plan to make a lengthy stop at the fascinating Shelburne Museum, seven miles south of Burlington. It's not anything like a stuffy, old-fashioned kind of indoor museum. Mr. & Mrs. J. Watson Webb created it in 1947, originally as a place to display family carriages and sleighs. Today there are 45 acres with 35 historic buildings exhibiting three centuries of Americana. Children will love it; so will you. The Museum is open May 15 to October 15, and visitors can explore a blacksmith's and wheelwright's shop, see a steam locomotive and the Lake Champlain sidewheeler steamer *Ticonderoga*, an old jail, a toy shop, general store, and loads more.

Burlington is Vermont's largest city, on the shore of gigantic Lake Champlain. Guns at Battery Park fought off British warships in the War of 1812. One-hour ferry rides take passengers across the lake to Port Kent, New York, in the summer months. And during July and August there are Mozart and Shakespeare festivals at various sites in and around town. At the University of Vermont's Robert Hull Fleming Museum, you can see an outstanding collection of European and Oriental art.

Out in Lake Champlain, just northwest of Burlington via Rte. 2, is a string of islands with several beautiful state parks. At Grand Isle visitors can explore the Hyde Log Cabin. Thought to be the oldest structure of its kind in the country, it was built in 1783 by Jedediah Hyde, Jr. For fishing enthusiasts, the waters off the south end of North Hero Island are highly recommended. And Isle La Motte is the site of Vermont's first white settlement, Fort Ste. Anne, constructed by the French in 1666.

Truax Tourist Home. It's on a quiet street in Burlington, near the University of Vermont, a simple house with porches and four rooms for guests. One bath is shared. Mrs. Effie A. Truax has been sharing her home with guests since the early 1940s. She says that her house is "just a comfortable place . . . and many folks come back for return visits."
32 University Terrace, Burlington, VT 05401; (802) 862-0809. Rates are inexpensive. Parking is available. Open all year.

Hedgemeer. Mrs. Grace D. Carlson is always pleased to greet travelers to the area. Her pleasant Colonial-design home is also near the University of Vermont and within walking distance of shops and restaurants. She has six guest rooms, each with TV and radio. Two of the rooms have their own lavatories; all of the rooms share three baths.
565 Main Street (Rte. 2), Burlington, VT 05401; (802) 862-5320. Rates are inexpensive. Parking is available. Open all year.

Charlie's Northland Lodge. This guest house is located on North Hero, one of the Lake Champlain islands. Charlie and Jorice Clark own and operate Northland Lodge, situated right in the heart of North Hero Village. It is a restored Colonial house, circa 1800-1850, with four double rooms for guests. Two have double beds, the others have twin beds, and two baths are shared. Separate guest cottages, fully furnished and electrically heated, are also available. There's a comfortable lounge in the main house for relaxing, and the Clarks offer their guests morning coffee and homemade doughnuts for a small extra charge. Restaurants and shops are within walking distance. If you enjoy fishing, Charlie's Northland Lodge is the place to come—even in fall or winter. Bass, walleye and great northern pike abound in Lake Champlain, and there's a fine sport and tackle shop on the premises. All baits are available in season; boats and motors may be rented. And if fishing doesn't excite you, there are plenty of other activities including pleasure boating and sailing, swimming and hiking. In addition, two professional tennis courts are on the lodge's grounds. In winter, thirty wooded acres offer eight to ten miles of groomed cross-country ski trails; skis may be rented.

Rte. 2, North Hero, VT 05474; (802) 372-8822. (On North Hero Island, 30 miles north of Burlington, 60 miles south of Montreal.) Rates are moderate, lower off season. Visa and MasterCard are accepted. No pets, please, and there are no rollaway beds for children. Open all year.

Side Trip to Stowe

SMUGGLERS' NOTCH/MT. MANSFIELD/STOWE

From Burlington, follow Rte. 15 and wend your way northeast to Jeffersonville. It's an excellent place to stay while you explore the area. One of my all-time favorite drives is through Smuggler's Notch, south of Jeffersonville on Rte. 108. During the War of 1812 goods were smuggled into Canada via this rugged gorge.

Today, if you're at all romantic, you may have the prickly feeling that a highwayman lurks behind every one of the enormous fallen boulders which lie beside the steep, twisting, narrow road. The black forest encroaches on each side as you creep along, and rock walls tower ominously above—it's a marvelously sinister mountain fastness.

Mt. Mansfield is Vermont's highest peak—4393 feet—and the toll road, south of Smuggler's Notch off Rte. 108, winds to its summit with impressive vistas at each turn. The road is open only in summer, weather permitting. You may, if you wish, ride a gondola up the mountain instead, leaving from the Spruce Peak Ski Area.

Stowe, a long-time summer and winter resort, lies in the valley below Mt. Mansfield at the junction of Rtes. 108 and 100. Settled in 1794, Stowe is beloved by skiers for the great abundance of snow that falls almost every year. The town offers visitors a wealth of shops, galleries and interesting restaurants.

Green Valley Guest Home. Ken and Ruth Nye's Green Valley in Jeffersonville is a white ranch house, set back from the road. Lots of flowers bloom in summertime, and a pleasant patio out back overlooks the garden and hillsides. Inside, there are five large guest rooms, sharing 2½ baths: one twin, two doubles, one with two double beds, and one single. The house is furnished in antiques, and the beds are covered with Ruth's handmade quilts. Guests are welcome to use the big living room for relaxing. Green Valley Guest Home is about four miles from restaurants and shops and eight miles from Mt. Mansfield.

Rte. 15, Jeffersonville, VT 05464; (802) 644-2969. (Between Jeffersonville and Johnson.) Rates are inexpensive. Open all year.

Stowe-Bound Lodge. An old New England house, this comfortable establishment was built around the 1830s. Dick and Erika Brackenbury have fourteen rooms for guests, four with private bath, the rest sharing five bathrooms. The Lodge is a pleasant place; guests can relax beside the fire in the sitting room, read in the library or sing around the piano. Eight acres of land surround the house; the Brackenburys have a small organic farm with a variety of animals including sheep, goats, cows and a horse. They also offer fiber to fabric wool craft, spinning, weaving and knitting. Continental or full breakfasts are served; dinners are available by advance reservation and include fruits and vegetables grown on the farm.

Rte. 100, Lower Village, Stowe, VT 05672; (802) 253-4515. Rates are moderate, higher if meals are included; group rates are available. Children are welcome, pets if leashed. Open all year.

Route 100—Waterbury to Wilmington

WATERBURY

Schneider Haus. Schneider Haus, near Waterbury, is a departure from most New England guest houses. It is a Tyrolean chalet, snugly nestled high on a hillside, far from the road. Goerge and Irene Ballschneider built the house after falling in love with similar homes in Austria and Germany. The exterior is authentically Austrian with sharply-pitched roof and railed balconies. Each of the ten guest rooms is furnished with antiques and handmade quilts. Five baths are shared; two rooms share a connecting bath. In summer, a private bath may be available. Guests are invited to enjoy the cozy lounge; its enormous stone fireplace was constructed by the owners in only 2½ weeks. Irene Ballschneider likes to tell her guests that she built one side and George the other, and ask which looks better! There is also a game room with ping-pong and pool tables.

Guest Houses

A full breakfast is included in the rates, served in a pretty, wood-paneled dining room. Zucchini or other breads are specialties, along with bacon and eggs or French toast, coffee, tea or hot chocolate. Afternoon tea and coffee are also served. A refrigerator is available for guests' use, and outdoors, barbecue grills for cookouts in summer. There are tennis courts, and even a small barn that houses a few animals. Schneider Haus is in the country, about five to fifteen minutes away from restaurants and shops, and the Sugarbush Ski Area is fifteen miles south.

Rte. 100, Duxbury, VT; (802) 244-7726. Mailing address: Box 283A, Waterbury, VT 05676. (Four miles south of Waterbury Village, five miles south of Exit 10 off I-89.) Rates are inexpensive, lower in winter. Visa, MasterCard and American Express are accepted. Children are welcome; no pets, please. Open July 1–November 1 and December 15–April 1.

MAD RIVER VALLEY/WARREN

Just south of Waterbury on Rte. 100 is one of the country's finest winter ski regions. Sugarbush, Glen Ellen and Mad River are located here. But thousands of people come to the area in other seasons; there are activities galore for every taste. Horseback riding over winding trails is a joy. You can swim in pools or in the clear, icy waters of a mountain stream, fish or canoe, either white-water or placid paddling. At the Sugarbush Airport, instructors will take you for a ride in a power plane, or better still, give you a soaring lesson. And if you are in Warren on the Fourth of July, don't miss its old-fashioned parade and fair.

For an unforgettable side trip, take Rte. 17 west at Waitsfield, up over the Appalachian Gap. You'll have to come back the same way, unless you want to join up with Rte. 116 or 7 on the other side. It is a fantastic drive, with ever-changing views of mountains—and more mountains. Sometimes in late fall the foliage still glows with color on the lower mountainsides, while the trees higher up are bare. With snow on the topmost peaks, and if a light mist has fallen, every twig and branch covered with ice—it's an incredible magic world of glittering crystal.

Birch Wood ... by the mountain. Originally their vacation home, Jack and Kathleen Horst's small chalet in Warren is now shared with paying guests. Birch Wood is built into a wooded hill, at the top of winding flagstone steps. Kathleen Horst says that many of their guests have become personal friends, and return time and time again—for skiing, soaring, the glorious fall foliage, or just to sit around the fireplace and chat over fresh apple cider and cheese. There are three rooms with double beds, sharing a bath, and a separate three-bedroom, two-bath chalet that sleeps eight. Breakfast is included in the rates—juice, eggs, waffles or cereal depending on the day, toast and coffee or tea. Three restaurants, a ski area, tennis courts, swimming, hiking trails and a golf course are all within walking distance. Reservations are strongly recommended for weekends, and a *must* for foliage season and winter.

German Flats Road, Box 80, Warren, VT 05674; (802) 583-2100. (Two miles off Rte. 100 on the road connecting Sugarbush Ski Area and Sugarbush North.) Rates are moderate; special mid-week rates are available. Open all year.

The Homestead. A good place for families or young people on ski vacations, The Homestead in East Warren is a rambling old country farmhouse. It's comfortable and homelike, and Mrs. Thelma Ricketts will tell you where the best mountain views and hiking trails may be found. She also provides a big, home-cooked country breakfast for a small extra charge, and if she doesn't have too many guests she might even fix dinner. There are ten guest rooms sleeping four to a room, sharing three baths with showers.

East Warren, VT 05674; (802) 496-3744. (Located 2½ miles east of Rte. 100, at junction of Roxbury Mountain Range connecting Rte. 100 in Warren to Rte. 12A in Roxbury.) Rates are inexpensive. Open all year.

PITTSFIELD/LUDLOW/PLYMOUTH

Continuing south on Rte. 100 you will come to Pittsfield, and shortly thereafter you'll see the signs for Pico Peak and Killington Ski Areas. The 3½-mile Gondola Tramway at Killington offers views of five states when you reach the top. Further on will be the town of Ludlow.

The first steam train came to Ludlow in 1849 and the valley soon had flourishing woolen mills, an iron foundry that produced wood stoves, and talc mines. Many of the streams back up in the hills still have mineral deposits of garnets and quartz—and even gold. For another grand panoramic view of the mountains and valley, drive up South Hill just out of the center of town.

Guest Houses

Round Top Mountain Ski Area is just north, near Plymouth, where Calvin Coolidge, 30th President of the United States, was born, grew up, took the oath of office and is buried. His old homestead is in Plymouth Notch, a mile north on Rte. 100A, as is the Farmers' Museum, an old barn with a large display of pre-1900 farming tools.

The locally famed Plymouth salute cannon was fired from the barn's doorway. Apparently this cannon was the cause of a great many fights between the "boys" of Plymouth Union and Plymouth Notch, both groups being determined to take possession. Calvin Coolidge's uncle, John Wilder, owned the barn. As Uncle John described the scene: "On the Fourth, after we had made the raid on the Union and dragged the cannon up the hill, we felt certain the boys would be back for it, so we posted a lookout at the top of the Notch.

"Meantime we fired the cannon and shook the window lights of the whole village. We had a strong rope hitched to the carriage of the gun, the other end being tied to a beam in the back of the barn. Every time we shot the cannon we'd pull it back into the barn, shut the doors and then swab it out and reload.

"But that wasn't all. Just as soon as the gun was pulled in we'd take up three planks in the barn floor next to the doors, so that if the Union crowd should get past the guard and made a rush they would fall through the opening into the cow stable below."

Makes you think, doesn't it? We modern folk don't know how to have fun anymore.

Colton Guest Farm. Set on a 200-acre farm, this homey country house is well over a century old. Mr. and Mrs. Robert F. Colton own the farm, and Mr. Colton was born in the old 22-room farmhouse. Nine of the rooms are for guests, two with three single beds in each, one with a double and two single beds, three each with one double bed, and three with twin beds. Four baths are shared. There's a living room/lounge with a fireplace, card table, games and bumper pool for guests to enjoy. Outdoors are a picnic table and fireplace, badminton and volleyball courts, and, located on the lower meadow, a private pond to swim in. The Coltons keep the house, furnished with some interesting family antiques, immaculately clean, and also maintain the grounds and garden in apple-pie order. Their eldest son helps with the maple

**Colton Guest Farm,
Pittsfield, Vermont**

sugaring in the spring. On the farm are a dozen cattle, and a blond German shepherd dog. Fishing, hunting, hiking and skiing are conveniently nearby. Guests are offered a home-cooked, country style breakfast year-round; from October to April, except on Friday nights, dinner is served.

Rte. 100, Pittsfield, VT 05762; (802) 746-8901. Rates are moderate; special weekend and ski week rates are available. Children are welcome; no pets, please, Open all year.

The Red Door. This small guest house in Ludlow is of early New England architecture, built in 1833. Mrs. Letty Whittemore has three attractive rooms for visitors, all with comfortable beds. The bath is shared. Guests are welcome to enjoy the cozy living room, too, with TV. Mrs. Whittemore does not serve meals but will recommend some excellent restaurants nearby. (Guests are invited to make coffee for themselves in the morning.) She will also tell you all about the things to see and do in the area, including antique shops, museums, parks and sports activities. The Red Door is one mile from Okemo Mountain Ski Area base lodge.

7 Pleasant Street, Ludlow, VT 05149; (802) 228-2376. (Almost directly behind the Post Office.) Rates are inexpensive. Children and pets are welcome. Open all year except one month during April and May.

WESTON/LONDONDERRY/GRAFTON

Weston, on Rte. 100, is another of Vermont's charming small villages, with a well-known summer theater right on the green and some interesting shops. It also has the famous Weston Bowl Mill which has been turning out bowls and other wooden items for more than three-quarters of a century.

Magic Mountain and Stratton Mountain Ski Areas are adjacent to the town of Londonderry. The Stratton Arts Festival is held each year mid-September to mid-October at Stratton Mountain Base Lodge. And you can take a ride on the chairlift up and down the mountain, if you like.

Picturesque Grafton is east of Londonderry, via Rte. 11 East and then 10 miles east on Rte. 121. For the most part, Rte. 121 is unpaved, so go slowly and expect to bounce a bit. It's fun though—and really backcountry. If you don't want to try it, follow Rte. 11 to Rte. 35 south. The drowsy, tiny town of Grafton is worth seeing; it doesn't appear to have changed much in a century or so, with its gracious white and mellow brick houses and old church.

The Darling Family Inn, Weston, Vermont

The Darling Family Inn. Wide floorboards, American and English country antiques and lots of copper, brass and pewter grace this 150-year-old converted farmhouse. Known as the Black Shutters Inn until 1981, it is now owned and operated by Chapin and Joan Darling. The handsome Colonial red house sits on three acres of land just outside Weston Village, with a magnificent view of the mountains. There are five double rooms for guests, including one with private bath; the others share two baths. (In addition, two completely furnished housekeeping cottages are on the grounds, insulated and heated for year-round use.) The rooms are charming, decorated with lovely period furniture and accessories, and colorful, locally-crafted quilts. A living room with fireplace is a nice spot to relax, and perhaps have a drink (BYOB) at the end of the day. Guests can fish 100 yards from the house, and there is a swimming pool, too. Excellent hiking trails are nearby, and both downhill and cross-country skiing are easily accessible. The fascinating Weston Priory is not far away. A continental breakfast is included in the rates for room guests; full breakfasts and packed lunches are available to both room and cottage guests for an extra charge. Joan Darling's special pancakes with Vermont maple syrup are rapidly becoming renowned. She also provides little surprises for guests staying in the main house—but you'll have to discover those for yourself!

Rte. 100, Weston, VT 05161; (802) 824-3223. (Half a mile from the village of Weston.) Rates are moderate; special weekly rates are available. MasterCard and Visa are accepted. No children under eight or pets in inn; both are welcome in cottages. Open all year.

**The Hayes House,
Grafton, Vermont**

The Hayes House. Mrs. Margery Hayes Heindel owns this 17th-century three-story farmhouse in Grafton. Comfortably furnished, it has four guest rooms: one double with private bath and a fireplace, two doubles sharing a bath, and one single sharing a bath. Guests may also use the family room with fireplace and color TV. Mrs. Heindel is a great gardener, with a large vegetable garden, smooth lawns and many flowers. She says there are two dogs and one cat as full-time residents besides herself; she is presently chairman of the Board of Selectmen. A continental breakfast of juice, homemade muffins and jelly or jam, coffee or tea is included in the rates. In wintertime, skiers are welcomed back from a day's run on the slopes with hot, homemade soup. The house is only a three-minute walk from Grafton village.

Bear Hill Road, Grafton, VT 05146; (802) 843-2461. (Located on Bear Hill Road where the north and south branches of Saxton's River meet and the road crosses a covered bridge to climb Bear Mountain.) Rates are moderate, slightly higher in winter with a fuel surcharge. Children and pets are welcome, but must stay with parents/owner. Open all year.

Woodchuck Hill Farm. One of the oldest farmhouses in Grafton (circa 1780), Woodchuck Hill is a handsome white Colonial, furnished in antiques. The view is superb; the house sits on a hilltop on 200 acres of farmland and you can see for 75 miles, all the way to Mt. Monadnock in New Hampshire. Anne and Frank Gabriel describe their house as "at the end of the road, perfect for those who love the peace and quiet of rural New England." Guests may walk through the fields or woods, swim in the Gabriels' own pond, or spend a restful afternoon just reading or dozing on the huge porch which overlooks the countryside. On cool evenings there is always a fire in one of the *five* fireplaces! There is TV for those who want it. Visitors are encouraged to make themselves right at home. The Gabriels run their own antique shop in the old barn. There are four single and double guest rooms, sharing two baths; a barn apartment and a studio apartment, both with kitchens. Afternoon tea or coffee is served at Woodchuck Hill, with an assortment of fancy breads, for a small extra charge; set-ups for beverages and wine are also provided for a nominal fee, accompanied by complimentary crackers and Grafton cheese. Dinners, at extra cost, are available by reservation.

Middletown Road, Grafton, VT 05146; (802) 843-2398. (Two miles west of Grafton village.) Room rates are moderate; apartments are higher. Children over seven are welcome; no pets, please. Open May 1–November 15.

WEST DOVER/WILMINGTON/MARLBORO

From Grafton, a scenic way back to Rte. 100 is to follow Rte. 35 south to Townshend and then Rte. 30 northwest. A stretch of 35 isn't paved, however, and lovely though back roads are, there are times when the heart sinks at seeing that sign ahead: "Unpaved road." You may, of course, consider it a test of character.

Way down at the end of Rte. 100, the Mount Snow Valley stretches alongside the southern ridge of Vermont's Green Mountains. Skiing is super in this region, with several ski areas to choose from, but it's also a fine summertime objective. Wilmington has a great many interesting shops and some excellent restaurants. Marlboro, internationally known for its annual music festival held each July and August, is a few twisty miles east of Wilmington on Rte. 9. Musicians come from all over to study here, and on weekends perform for the public. You need to reserve tickets in advance, though, if you want to attend a concert.

Snow Den Inn. Milt and Jean Cummings welcome guests year-round to their century-old Vermont farmhouse in West Dover, six miles north of Wilmington. The house, recently redecorated, has six double rooms for guests, all with private baths. Many of the rooms have antique furnishings; handmade quilts cover the beds. A cozy den offers TV, a library, and a marvelous view of the mountains. Skiing, of course, is available nearby in winter. In summer, activities in the area include a gondola ride to the top of Mt. Snow, swimming, boating, golfing and tennis. A full breakfast and lunch are served, if you want, for an extra charge. Restaurants and shops are within walking distance.

Rte. 100, P.O. Box 615, West Dover, VT 05356; (802) 464-9355. Rates are moderate, and vary according to the season. Visa and MasterCard accepted. Children are welcome; no pets, please. Open all year.

The Weathervane Lodge. A charming Tyrolean-style lodge, the Weathervane is also located in West Dover, and also offers a grand, panoramic view of the mountains. Liz and Ernie Chabot are your hosts, and have ten rooms for guests, plus a suite and a two-bedroom apartment. Two of the rooms have private baths; the others share six baths. Guests enjoy the lounge and recreation rooms with fireplaces, color TV, piano, ping-pong table and a set-up bar (BYOB). For winter guests, the Chabots provide free cross-country ski equipment, a toboggan, sleds and snowshoes. In the summer, a raft of activities are available including badminton, volleyball, water sports of all kinds and horseback riding. Breakfast is served year-round, included in the rates. In winter, dinner (except on Friday nights) is also included.

Rte. 100, West Dover, VT 05356; (802) 464-5426. (About six miles north of Wilmington; follow the signs to the Weathervane.) Rates are moderate, lower in summer; special holiday, weekend and ski week rates are available. MasterCard and Visa are accepted. Children are welcome; no pets, please. Open all year.

The Nutmeg Inn. In 1957 this 200-year-old Vermont farmhouse was restored and remodeled into a comfortable guest house. Joan and Rich Combes are the cordial hosts, along with their two children, Ed and Cindi. The house is painted a cheerful red with white shutters, and is situated at a bend in the road across from a river. In summer, flowers bloom colorfully all around the house. There are nine guest rooms, pleasantly furnished. In winter, bunk beds are added to some rooms, perfect for families. Four of the rooms have private baths; the others share two baths. The old carriage house is now a lounge with fireplace, piano, TV, games and books, and a BYOB bar. In summer and fall the Combeses serve a full country breakfast, included in the rates. In winter, the rates include both breakfast and dinner, featuring delicious "country style" home cooking.

Rte. 9 West (Molly Stark Trail), Wilmington, VT 05363; (802) 464-3351. (One mile west of Wilmington's traffic light.) Rates are moderate; special weekly rates are available in winter. No children under 9 and no pets, please. Open Memorial Day–end of October, and December–mid-April.

Route 12, Montpelier South to Woodstock

MONTPELIER

Montpelier, on the Winooski River, is the capital of Vermont, nestled in the midst of the Green Mountains. Somehow this city always surprises me . . . the gold leaf-covered dome of the State House looks charmingly incongruous gleaming brightly against the tree-covered hills. Perhaps it's just that one doesn't expect a city here. The State House itself is a classic small example of Greek revival architecture, constructed of Vermont granite with soaring Doric columns.

Adjacent to the State House is the Vermont Historical Society Museum and Library. It has some excellent exhibits, including a fascinating one on the 14-year period when Vermont was an independent Republic (1777-1791).

Lackey's Tourist Home. Richard and Sally Donaghy own this handsome old brick mansion in Montpelier. It is an 1890 Victorian house, with every bit of that era's original atmosphere preserved—knicknacks and all. The capitol building is only a short walk away, as are the Historical Museum, restaurants and stores. The house has a broad front porch for sitting, and a nice lawn with lots of shade trees. Nine comfortable rooms are available for guests, sharing four baths.
152 State Street (Rte. 2), Montpelier, VT 05602; (802) 223-7292. Rates are inexpensive. Open all year.

NORTHFIELD/RANDOLPH
Northfield is a nice little town. Since 1866 it has been the home of Norwich University, now a coeducational college. America's first private military academy, the school was founded in Norwich, Vermont, in 1819.

The Randolph area offers golf, swimming, fishing, horseback riding and terrific skiing, all within three miles of the town.

MacKenzie Tourists. Mrs. Joan MacKenzie owns this 1955 ranch-style house in Northfield Center, across the road from Norwich University. It's a red house with white trim. She has two, sometimes three rooms for guests with single or double beds, and usually prefers two persons per room. One bath, with shower, is shared. No smoking, alcoholic beverages or food are allowed in the rooms. There is a living room with TV and a lawn out back with a few lawn chairs. A ramp wheelchair entrance leads through the back door. Guests are offered complimentary coffee or tea on arrival. Parents of university students often stay here, and the young people can visit, and share pie or other homebaked goodies in the dining room. Several restaurants and a number of shops are within a mile of the house, and the Norwich University Ski Area is nearby.
9 Stagecoach Road, Northfield Center, VT 05663; (802) 485-7343. (From I-89 take Exit 5 to Rte. 12, north to the Texaco Station and it's the next road on the right—about four miles.) Rates are inexpensive. No pets, please. Open all year.

Guest Houses

Windover House. Built in 1800 and restored in 1960, Windover House in Randolph is a comfortably furnished, friendly guest house owned by George and Shirley Carlisle. It's a large white structure with a wonderfully wide, long porch, set on five acres of wooded countryside with some of the oldest trees in the state. There are eight guest bedrooms, two with private baths, the others sharing three bathrooms. Guests may use the spacious living room with its lovely bowed window, fireplace, piano and color TV. Windover House is only one mile from shops and restaurants, and is about 25 miles from either Woodstock or Montpelier. The Green Mountain Ski Touring Center is five minutes away, and the house is halfway between Stowe and Killington for downhill skiing. The Carlisles serve guests a continental breakfast or a full breakfast, for a small extra charge. Coffee and tea are available at all times.

Randolph Center Road, Randolph, VT 05060; (802) 728-3802. (From I-89 take Exit 4; follow the sign to Randolph. You will now be on Rte. 66; Windover House is two miles down Rte. 66 at corner of Rtes. 66 and 12.) Rates are inexpensive to moderate. Children are welcome; pets are, too, if they stay outside. Open all year.

WOODSTOCK/WINDSOR

Further south on Rte. 12 you'll come to Woodstock, one of Vermont's most visited villages. It is an extremely attractive town set in the foothills of the Green Mountains, with many lovely old houses, a village green and covered bridges. The Ottauquechee River runs right through the middle of Woodstock; several good ski areas are nearby (Mt. Tom and Suicide Six) and there are many excellent horseback riding trails. The town also offers a goodly number of interesting shops and restaurants.

Visit the Woodstock Historical Society on Elm Street, and wander around admiring the large, handsome homes in the historic district. Twenty years after the first settler arrived in 1765, Woodstock became the Shire Town, or seat of Windsor County. It was a thriving central business and political district for a time, with many stores and small industries—and five weekly newspapers!

Woodstock's population declined in the late 1800s, but its popularity did not. Nowadays it's a year-round lure for tourists and skiers. The very first rope tow up a mountain was constructed here in 1934, an unassuming start for a giant industry.

From Woodstock, Rte. 12 leads you east and then south to

Hartland; Rte. 5 south takes you to Windsor, right on the Vermont/New Hampshire border. America's longest covered bridge (460 feet) spans the Connecticut River between the two states. Built in 1866, it is still very much in use.

Settled in 1764, Windsor is where Vermont's constitution was drawn up and signed in 1777. The delegates were gathered and working busily away when postriders raced up to warn them of trouble at Ticonderoga. They wanted to adjourn immediately to defend their homes, but a monumental thunderstorm held them captive. So, being typical Yankees and not inclined to waste time, they voted to adopt their new constitution—and then went off to fight. From May 15 to October 15 you can visit the Constitution Museum on Main Street. Open year-round is Windsor House, a beautifully restored 1840 building, once a hotel. Items made by more than 200 Vermont craftspeople are on display.

Cambria House. A six-minute walk from Woodstock village, Cambria House was built around 1880, and is furnished in period style. Its five large guest rooms share two baths, and there is a comfortable living room with TV and reading library for guests to enjoy. The big yellow house with black shutters is owned by Eugene Higgins, and is right beside the road, with a hill rising up behind. No food is served, but several excellent restaurants are within easy walking distance.
43 Pleasant Street (Rte. 4), Woodstock, VT 05091; (802) 457-3077. Rates are inexpensive. Parking is available in back. Children and pets are welcome by pre-arrangement. Open all year except from June 1–15.

Three Church Street, Bed and Breakfast. Eleanor C. Paine welcomes guests to her handsome Woodstock home, listed in the National Historic Registry. The original brick part of the house was built in the 1820s; added to from time to time it now has 25 rooms. As Mrs. Paine puts it: "The architecture is a mish-mash of Federal, New Orleans, and two new contemporary rooms." A bust of the Marquis de Lafayette may be seen in a hall niche; it has been there for at least 50 years—and as the Marquis did visit Woodstock in 1825, it's suggested that he may have stayed in the house. In more recent years, Mrs. Paine's eight children were raised there. Now that half of them are out on their own, she decided it was an appropriate time to open the doors to guests looking for the distinctive "Bed and Breakfast" experience popular in

Guest Houses

Europe. And although her house presents a somewhat elegant facade, Mrs. Paine and her family create a delightfully informal and relaxing atmosphere.

There are ten double rooms for guests, one with private bath. Included in these there can be one two-room suite with small kitchen, and two three-room suites, one with kitchen, the other with toaster oven, refrigerator and hot plate. The suites are available only by the week or weekend. All of the rooms are different, and decorated individually with at least one piece of antique furniture or art work; antiques are liberally scattered throughout the house. Guests are invited to enjoy the formal music room, cozy library, spacious living and dining rooms, and gallery overlooking the Ottauquechee River and Mt. Tom. Outdoors are a swimming pool and clay tennis court for guests' pleasure.

Now for a description of breakfast at Three Church Street. You'll enjoy just reading about it! Mrs. Paine quotes Nathaniel Hawthorne on the subject: "Life, within doors, has few pleasanter prospects than a neatly arranged and well provisioned breakfast table"—and she has obviously taken these words to heart. Breakfast, included in the rates, offers a selection of juices, hot cereals, sausage, bacon, ham, corn beef hash, chicken livers, home fries and grits. In addition, one may choose eggs cooked in a variety of ways, omelets, pancakes or French toast. And pastries. On Sunday your hostess outdoes herself with eggs Benedict or blueberry pancakes. Throughout the day or night instant coffee, tea, hot chocolate and soups are available.

For other meals, Woodstock has a number of fine restaurants within easy walking distance of Three Church Street. Boutiques, antique shops and historic houses are close by; golf, horseback riding, fishing and hiking are easily accessible. Silver Lake, six miles away, offers a fine beach; the Country Club (open to the public) with golf, tennis and cross-country skiing, is a half mile away. For downhill skiing there is Killington (a 40-minute drive) plus five other major ski areas within an hour's drive.

3 Church Street, Woodstock, VT 05091; (802) 457-1925. (In the village on Rte. 4 immediately west of the Town Hall/Movie Theater.) Rates are moderate. MasterCard and Visa are accepted. Children are welcome; extra cots and cribs are available. Well-mannered pets, too, are allowed but must be confined to bedrooms when not outdoors. Parking is available at the house. Open May 1–November 1 and December 15–March 15.

What Not House. Four acres of beautiful grounds surround this nice old guest house, located on Rte. 5 just before you reach the town of Windsor. From the gardens there's a marvelous view of the mountains. Mrs. R. L. Henry can accommodate 18 guests in her antique-filled home, in eight bedrooms sharing six baths. She doesn't serve breakfast, but there are many fine places to eat not far away. The What Not House is very popular and busy, so Mrs. Henry recommends that guests make reservations ahead of time if possible. You'll enjoy meeting your remarkable hostess, by the way. A Vermont native who has traveled widely, Mrs. Henry turned 93 in the fall of 1981 and is still going strong. She has some grand tales to tell about her long and active life and her travels, and she'll be delighted to share some of them with you. Ask to see the guest book at What Not House, too: visitors have come here from all over the world!

North Main Street (Rte. 5), Windsor, VT 05089; (802) 674-5574. Rates are inexpensive. Open May–November; at other times of the year, call and ask.

Rte. 2, Montpelier east to St. Johnsbury and south on Rte. 5

Side Trip To Barre

East of Montpelier, a short side trip on Rte. 14 South off Rte. 2 will bring you to Barre and The Rock of Ages Quarry and Craftsman Center. See the awesome granite quarries, 350- to 400-foot-deep canyons—and watch them being worked. Free guided tours are available from May to October.

ST. JOHNSBURY

St. Johnsbury is approximately 90 miles east of Montpelier, about halfway between the Green Mountains of Vermont and New Hampshire's White Mountains. Vermont is known for its maple syrup industry, and in St. Johnsbury you can see how it works, from start to finish.

The Maple Grove Museum with its authentic sugar house is on the eastern edge of the city, on Rte. 2. It's open from Memorial Day to Late October, Monday through Friday, except holidays. Tours are given of the Maple Grove candy factory all year, and yes—you do get samples!

Some of Vermont's loveliest lakes lie in the region north of St. Johnsbury. Lake Willoughby (follow Rte. 5 and then 5A north) is one of the most striking. Mt. Pisgah, a sheer, stark, glacier-cut cliff towers 2600 feet above one side. With Mt. Hor on the other; the area really looks more Scandinavian or Swiss than New England. The deep, cold waters offer great fishing.

Sherryland. Mr. and Mrs. Henry Sherry own this beautifully restored New England farmhouse near St. Johnsbury. There are five large, light guest rooms, sharing a bath, and a warm, homey atmosphere throughout. Meals are not included, but Mrs. Sherry sometimes provides breakfast for an extra charge. The house is located approximately half a mile from several good restaurants.

Joes Brook Road, Danville, VT 05828; (802) 684-3354. (One-half mile south of Danville Village just west of St. Johnsbury.) Rates are inexpensive. No pets, please. Open all year.

Echo Ledge Farm. The farm, located in East St. Johnsbury, was first settled in 1793. Today, owners Larry Greenwood, his Scottish wife, Rosina, and their son, raise Simmental cattle and operate a guest house. Mrs. Greenwood teaches, too, besides canning and freezing great quantities of homegrown vegetables. Many of their guests return year after year to enjoy the friendly, easy-going country farm ambiance. Four of the guest rooms have private baths; the others share two baths. There is a separate central lounge for reading or watching color cable TV. No meals are served, but there are many good places to eat in town, and the Greenwoods will be happy to recommend some.

Rte. 2, P.O. Box 77, East St. Johnsbury, VT 05838; (802) 748-4750. (Five and a half miles east of St. Johnsbury.) Rates are inexpensive to moderate. Well-behaved children and pets are welcome. Open June–October.

BRADFORD/FAIRLEE/POST MILLS/ NORTH THETFORD/CHELSEA

From St. Johnsbury, you could take I-91 south all the way to the Massachusetts border. But Rte. 5 south runs almost parallel with I-91 and is much to be preferred if you have the time. The road follows along the smooth-flowing Connecticut River, through gently rolling hills and past green pastures and woods. Down beyond the town of Bradford are Lakes Morey and Fairlee, both popular resort areas. A bit further you'll come to North Thetford. For an interesting side trip from either North

Thetford or Post Mills on Lake Fairlee, take Rte. 113 north and west to Chelsea. Another attractive small Vermont village, Chelsea, situated at the junction of Rtes. 113 and 110, is well off the beaten path. Back on Rte. 5 you will arrive at Norwich. Here, if you like, you can cross over the river into Hanover, New Hampshire . . . or continue south on 5 to Massachusetts.

Merry Meadow Farm, Bradford, Vermont

Merry Meadow Farm. Set on more than 100 acres of fields, woodlands and hills partially bordering the Connecticut River, Merry Meadow Farm in Bradford specializes in horses and horseback riding. In July and August, the farm is a riding school for children. But throughout the rest of the year, Merry Meadow welcomes guests of all ages.

Jack and Betty Williams and their family operate this unique establishment. It is a working farm, and guests are invited —if they like—to help with the farm chores, which might include haying or gardening. Unlimited horseback riding is included in the rates; there are 56 well-schooled horses. Lessons are available. The farm has its own indoor arena, cross-country course and miles of beautiful trails. Guests may also hike, canoe, swim in the river or in Merry Meadow's pool, take a hay or sleigh ride (depending on the season), square dance, or enjoy one of the many indoor and outdoor games available. Dartmouth College in Hanover is only fifteen minutes away for theater, concerts, special events and downhill skiing.

There are eight guest rooms including four with double beds, two with twins and two singles, sharing four baths. One of the oldest households in Bradford, the farmhouse was built in 1834. Its decor is early American; bedrooms are furnished with antiques. Guests are invited to use two sitting rooms, both with fireplaces, one with TV. You may stay at the farm without meals, request individual meals only (such as just breakfast), or enjoy three homecooked meals per day, all served in the cozy farmhouse kitchen with its beamed ceiling and wood-burning stove. Coffee and tea are available at any time.

Lower Plain, Rte. 5, Bradford, VT 05033; (802) 222-4412. (From I-91, take Exit 6; go east on Rte. 25 for ¼-mile to intersection with Rte. 5; go south on 5 for 1½ miles and Merry Meadow will be on the right.) Rates are moderate and depend on number of meals you choose. Older children are welcome; younger ones must be supervised, especially around the animals. No pets, please. Open for adults and families September through June; for children only during July and August.

Aloha Manor, Fairlee, Vermont

Aloha Manor. Just a few miles south of Bradford, travelers will come to the scenic Lake Morey area. Aloha Manor is located right on the lake. The main house, now in its third location, is about 200 years old, and is owned and operated by Mrs. Helen Pierce Swetland. A long porch connects the house with the "Hearth," originally a horse barn and now used as a common room. A second barn houses "Early Attic Antiques." Set on more than 140 acres of lovely Vermont countryside, Aloha Manor offers all forms of water sports plus tennis, basketball and volleyball courts, swings, hiking and fishing. It has its own float, boats, canoes and beach. The large old farmhouse offers fifteen rooms for guests including three singles, ten doubles and two triples, furnished with comfortable antiques. All but two of the rooms have a private bath. There are, in addition, a number of cottages on the grounds. The "Aloha" name, by the way, was inherited from Mrs. Swetland's grandparents, who were born in Hawaii. Her great-grandparents were among those early medical missionaries who persuaded the Hawaiian natives to wear clothes! The now ubiquitous muumuu was created, Mrs. Swetland says, by her great-grandmother who possessed a sewing machine and only one pattern. Breakfasts are served at Aloha Manor on request, and there are many excellent restaurants within an eight-mile radius.

Lake Morey, Fairlee, VT 05045; (802) 333-4478. (Two and one-fourth miles east from Fairlee exit off I-91.) Rates are moderate. Children are welcome. Open June through October; some cottages are open year-round by lease.

The Lake House, Thetford, Vermont

The Lake House. Continuing south along Rte. 5 from Fairlee, a jog westward on delightfully scenic Rte. 244 along Lake Fairlee will bring you to Post Mills. The Lake House, owned by Ralph and Lea Easton, is located in the village of Post Mills, just 400 feet from the lake. The nice old house was built around 1865, and operated as a hotel for many years. The Eastons took it over in 1979. They have six guest bedrooms including one single and five doubles, sharing three full baths. For guests' use there are both open and screened porches, a living room with fireplace, and outdoors, lovely grounds with lawn furniture for sitting and sunning. All manner of activities are included in the rates, and evening tea, coffee and hot chocolate are also available. There are several good restaurants within eight miles.

Rte. 244, P.O. Box 65, Post Mills, VT 05058; (802) 333-4025. Rates are moderate. Visa and MasterCard are accepted. No pets, please. Open all year.

Stone House Inn. Located in North Thetford, this is an old stone farmhouse built in 1835 on the banks of the Connecticut River. Art and Dianne Sharkey are your hosts, and have four rooms for guests, all doubles. (Rooms may also be rented as singles.) Two baths are shared. Guests are welcome to use two sitting rooms, both with fireplaces; in summer, the large screened porch is a pleasant place to sit. The house is nicely furnished, partly with antiques. Outdoors are lawns, a pond and woods for walking. There is a public boat landing on the river next to the house, and the Sharkeys will plan a four-day canoe trip for you, if you like. Downhill skiing is only seven miles away and cross-country skiing is available right in North Thetford. A continental breakfast is included in the rates. On Friday and Saturday nights dinner is served, by advance reservations and at extra cost. The house also has a full liquor license. During the summer, meals are served on the porch overlooking the river.

Rte. 5, North Thetford, VT 05054; (802) 333-9124. Rates are moderate. Children are welcome; no pets, please. Open all year.

Shire Inn, Chelsea, Vermont

Shire Inn. Fred Sisser III is the genial host of the Shire Inn, one of Vermont's choicest bed and breakfast guest houses. Located in Chelsea, the exceptionally handsome 14-room brick house was built in 1832. Note the striking fanlight with its sunburst pattern over the front door, the spacious center hall, wide floorboards and spiral staircase. The doors have the original brass locks. There are four guest bedrooms: two queen-size and two with two double beds. The former share one bath, the other two each have a private bath. All are corner rooms and each has its own working fireplace. The house is decorated with period antiques, and guests are welcome to use the large, antique-filled living room with a fireplace, extensive library and windows on three sides. There's also a spacious porch. Shire Inn is set on 17 acres of land, through which runs a trout stream. A bridge over the stream leads to rolling hills (ideal for cross-country skiing in winter) and a forest beyond (for hiking in the summer). The grounds include many big old sugar maples, a formal garden with brick path and an antique shop. Breakfast is included in the rates, and consists of fruit in season, eggs, pancakes, locally-made bread, jelly, syrup and honey, and coffee, tea or milk. Restaurants and shops are within walking distance.

South Main Street (Rte. 110), Chelsea, VT 05038; (802) 685-3031. (In the village, off Town Green.) Rates are moderate. Children are welcome; no pets, please. Open all year.

The Lothrop Merry House, Vineyard Haven, Massachusetts

Bradford Gardens Inn, Provincetown, Massachusetts

Massachusetts

It's an oddly-shaped state, Massachusetts, like a rectangular elephant without legs. Cape Cod is the trunk, curving out and upwards. Despite its relatively small size, the state contains enough scenic and historic areas to keep a visitor busy for a lifetime. The population is dense around Massachusetts' larger cities, yet there are great stretches where one may drive long distances through almost uninhabited countryside.

Everyone knows about the Pilgrims and their arrival on the *Mayflower* in 1620. John Cabot (actually Giovanni Caboto) sailed south along the coast in 1498. The Norwegian adventurer Leif Ericson may also have explored New England's coast much earlier, around the year 1000. In the late 1800s and early 1900s the state hummed with mill industry; in recent years electronics have taken over.

The low, rolling hills of the Berkshires in the western part of Massachusetts have long lured summer vacationers, and today, winter skiers, too. Tanglewood, home of the Berkshire Music Festival, attracts thousands of music-lovers every summer. The west-central part of the state, through which flows the Connecticut River, is farming land.

Just outside of Boston in the east, Concord and Lexington welcome tourists year-round. Both towns have been very successful in preserving their Colonial past. It is not at all difficult for a visitor to feel as though he is reliving those events of two hundred years ago when the local farmers took on the seemingly invincible British.

Boston, Massachusetts' capital, is a walkable city where history jumps out at you at every turn. It is a city of scholars and politicians, of museums and seafood restaurants, and of ancient burying grounds resting in the shadow of ultramodern architecture. The old waterfront, including the fascinating Faneuil Hall Marketplace, is a gem of renovation attracting thousands of visitors each year.

Boston is also a city of confusing, narrow, one-way streets and eccentric motorists. Even the natives have problems navigating by car. If you can, stay outside—in Concord or on the North Shore, for instance, and take a train in. You'll be glad you did.

The best way to see Boston is on foot. Walk through the impeccable grounds of the old Public Garden and, in summer, take a ride on a Swanboat. These charmers have been operated by the same family for more than 100 years. Then cross the Common, once the colony's cow pasture and training field. Hike up to Beacon Hill with its steep, narrow streets, brick sidewalks and handsome old houses—and the State House with its golden dome.

At the red-brick information booth back down on the Common (on Tremont St. near the corner of Park St.) you can pick up a free brochure describing Boston's Freedom Trail. Follow the Trail down to the waterfront, paying a visit on the way to the Old Granary Burying Ground where so many early patriots lie, including Paul Revere, John Hancock and Samuel Adams. Still further down you will come to Faneuil Hall. Just beyond, three huge, long buildings have been turned into a colorful, bustling marketplace for ethnic foods of every kind, delightful shops and fine restaurants.

One shop in the Market sells nothing but toy bears; another has pigs in every imaginable form (except live). There's a bookshop just for children, and one that sells nothing but cookbooks of all kinds. A candy store offers countless flavors of jelly beans. Musicians and magicians entertain the throngs outdoors and there are plenty of benches to sit on while resting sore feet.

Along the waterfront are the New England Aquarium, boats for sightseeing cruises and more shops and places to eat. Old warehouses have been turned into expensive apartments; there are boat-filled marinas—and always, the salt-tanged air of the sea. Not far away in Charlestown (over the bridge) you can visit the USS *Constitution*, "Old Ironsides." She was built in 1797, and is still a commissioned ship of the U.S. Navy.

The North End, Boston's genuinely Italian neighborhood, is a brief walk up the hill behind the waterfront. Italian restaurants and bakeries full of luscious pastries dot the area. Here, also, are Paul Revere's House, Boston's oldest, and the Old North Church. From its steeple, the famed lanterns flashed to send Revere and William Dawes off on their famous midnight ride to warn the colonists the British were coming.

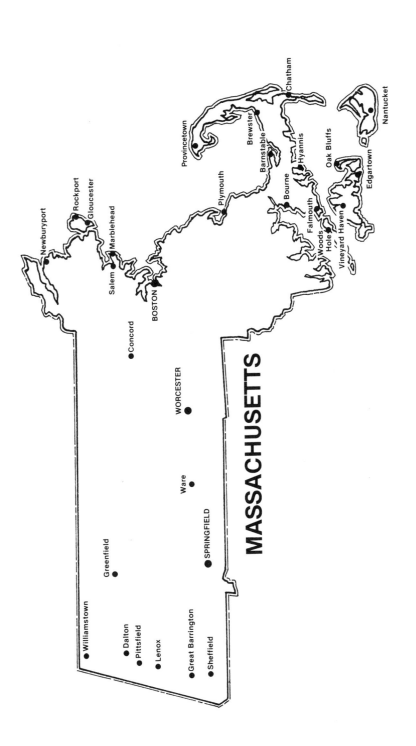

MASSACHUSETTS

Williamstown

Dalton
Pittsfield

Lenox

Great Barrington

Sheffield

Greenfield

SPRINGFIELD

Ware

WORCESTER

Concord

Newburyport

Rockport
Gloucester

Salem
Marblehead

BOSTON

Plymouth

Provincetown

Brewster

Barnstable

Bourne

Falmouth
Woods
Hole
Vineyard Haven

Hyannis

Oak Bluffs

Edgartown

Chatham

Nantucket

Guest Houses

Harvard and M.I.T. are in Cambridge, across the Charles River. Walk through venerable Harvard Yard and explore Harvard Square's multitude of shops and coffeehouses; it's a lively, collegiate scene.

North of Boston, dozens of quaint, hilly little towns cling to the rocky coastline. They're almost unbelievably picturesque, and great fun to wander through. Salem has its indelible history of witch hunts, lots of 17th-century houses, and a colorful waterfront area of intriguing shops. Gloucester, even today, is the home port for a thriving fishing industry. Marblehead and Rockport overflow with art galleries and, in summer, wall-to-wall tourists.

Driving along the South Shore of Massachusetts, one sees marshes, tiny islands, wealthy communities with impressive homes, and miles of beaches along the indented shoreline. Then the traveler crosses the bridge to Cape Cod, a different world entirely . . . of scrub pine and rolling sand dunes. In spring and early summer the Cape is a mass of wild roses and honeysuckle. Midsummer it's a mass of humanity, as towns fill up and almost burst with vacationers. In fall the cranberry bogs are red with fruit, and in winter the Cape reverts to its own sandy silence. Offshore are "the islands"—Martha's Vineyard and Nantucket, each with its own distinctive quality.

The Cape and South Shore usually enjoy mild winters with little snow. Inland the temperatures rise higher in summer and drop lower in winter. In spring apple blossoms froth in countless orchards, and in autumn the scent of ripe apples, Concord grapes and woodsmoke fills the air. Great mounds of orange pumpkins seem to be everywhere; farmstands selling pumpkins, squash and fresh apple cider dot the landscape in vast numbers. Even on rainy days the brilliant foliage seems to light up the countryside as though the sun were shining. In December, Massachusetts' small towns turn into live Christmas cards. Balsam wreaths hang on almost every door, candles glow from windows and Christmas trees twinkle brightly.

Massachusetts offers a great many guest houses. In some areas, such as Provincetown out at the end of Cape Cod and on the islands of Nantucket and Martha's Vineyard, guest houses outnumber motels and are *the* places to stay.

The Southern Berkshires
THE TANGLEWOOD REGION

This entire area is one big cultural festival, offering a fantastic variety of art, music, dance and theater. In addition, it abounds in pretty country roads and quiet little villages. Lenox, Stockbridge, and Great Barrington are all just a few miles off I-90, the Massachusetts Turnpike.

Tanglewood, at Lenox, would be a lovely place to visit even without music. The enormous Music Shed and other buildings are situated on a beautiful 210-acre estate in the green hills of western Massachusetts. Tanglewood is the summer home of the Boston Symphony Orchestra, with a full program of concerts beginning each July. You can listen to the music inside the Shed or recline lazily on the grass outside, sipping wine, gazing at the stars, and—at times—swatting mosquitoes. (Nothing is ever *quite* perfect.)

In nearby Becket the Jacob's Pillow Dance Festival offers everything from ballet to folk dancing each summer. North of Lenox, you can visit the Hancock Shaker Village (on Rte. 20 five miles west of Pittsfield) where some of that celibate sect settled in the late 1700s. The round stone barn and other restored buildings may be toured. Stockbridge, a charming town, was the home of the late Norman Rockwell; much of his delightfully nostalgic work may be seen at the Old Corner House.

Great Barrington, on Rte. 7 south of Stockbridge, puts on a real country fair every September; it has been held each year for more than a century. The town also opens many of its gracious old houses to the public, and there are loads of antique and craft shops.

During Tanglewood's summer music festival it is *very* difficult to find a place to stay, so try and make reservations as far in advance as you can. Also, many places require a minimum stay of three days, especially on weekends.

Ivanhoe Country House. Located on Rte. 41 near Sheffield, just south of Great Barrington, this beautiful old white Colonial house was built in 1780. It is situated right at the foot of Mt. Race on 25 acres of woods and lawns. The decor is appropriately comfortable country style, with lots of antiques and fireplaces. For guests, owners Carole and Dick Maghery have four rooms with private baths, three rooms sharing one

Guest Houses

Ivanhoe Country House, Sheffield, Massachusetts

bath, and a two-bedroom unit with private bath. Several of the rooms have working fireplaces; some have kitchenettes. Guests are invited to use the pleasant Chestnut Room, also with a fireplace. It includes a library, TV, piano, and ping-pong and game tables. Four refrigerators are available for keeping perishables, wine, beer or soft drinks. Outdoors, in addition to roaming the extensive grounds, guests may enjoy a swim in the pool or admire the Magherys' dogs—they raise golden retrievers.

A continental breakfast of muffins, coffee, tea or cocoa is included in the rates, and is even brought to your door in the morning! The Ivanhoe is not far from a number of excellent restaurants and interesting antique shops. Golf and tennis facilities are easily accessible at the public Egremont Country Club, downhill skiing at Catamount and Butternut Ski Basin, and cross-country skiing at Riverrun. Your hosts will be delighted to give you directions for all of these, plus the Appalachian Trail, Race Brook Falls, Bartholomew's Cobble—and, of course—Tanglewood, Jacobs Pillow and the Berkshire Playhouse.

Rte. 41, Undermountain Road, Sheffield, MA 01257; (413) 229-2143. Rates are moderate. Children are welcome. Because of the golden retrievers, the Magherys suggest you don't bring a pet of your own. If you do, the dog must be leashed and accompanied whenever away from your room, and walked away from the lawns. Open all year.

Elling's Guest House. Tall shade trees surround this beautiful old home in Great Barrington—a white Colonial built in 1746 by Stephen King, a wealthy woolen mill owner. There are six guest rooms, two with private baths and four sharing two full baths. Guests are invited to use the fireplaced parlor and the porch; the latter offers marvelous country and mountain views. Hosts Josephine (Jo) and Ray Elling serve breakfast —hot biscuits, jelly and jam, tea or coffee, included in the rates.
250 Maple Ave., RD 3, Box 6; Great Barrington, MA 01230; (413) 528-4103. (One mile west of Rte. 7.) Rates are moderate. No pets, please. Open all year.

Seekonk Pines. Linda and Chris Best are the proprietors of Seekonk Pines, another attractive Colonial guest house in Great Barrington. The place was built over 100 years ago, originally as the main house of a large estate. Upstairs are five bedrooms for guests, sharing two full baths, plus one large suite with private bath. Another room downstairs also has a private bath. Guests are welcome to use the spacious living room, with fireplace. Linda is an artist and framer, and the walls of the house are covered with her collection. Both Linda and Chris sing, and guests occasionally are treated to surprise recitals! Seekonk Pines is close to ski areas and all summer activities at Tanglewood, Jacobs Pillow and the like, and a swimming pool is on the grounds. A continental breakfast is included in the rates: homebaked bread or muffins, coffee, tea and juice. For an extra charge guests may indulge in a full breakfast of eggs or pancakes, bacon or sausage, plus those delicious homemade breads. In the late summer and fall, fresh produce from the garden is available for purchase.
Rte. 23 West and Seekonk Cross Road, Box 29AA, RD 1, Great Barrington, MA 01230; (413) 528-4192. (Two miles from Great Barrington.) Rates are moderate. Children are welcome but must be supervised by an adult; no pets, please. Open all year.

The Zuccos'. Angelo and Mary Zucco don't call their house in Great Barrington a "guest house," but they do welcome travelers on weekends and occasionally during the week. They have two double rooms and one single available, sharing a bath. Their house is on a quiet, attractive street, with an open front porch and back yard where there are lawn chairs for relaxing. There is a picnic table, too, and lovely flowers.

Guest Houses

Downtown Great Barrington is three-quarters of a mile away. *Fairview Terrace, RFD 2, Box 6, Great Barrington, MA 01230; (413) 528-1579. Rates are inexpensive. Children are welcome; no pets, please. Open May through October.*

Whistler's Inn. Located right in Lenox, this is a splendid old place—a rambling mansion built in 1820, a combination of French Manor and English Tudor architecture. The house originally belonged to the nephew of artist James McNeill Whistler, hence the name. Today Mr. and Mrs. Richard C. Mears are the owners. Richard Mears, a Baltimore native who divides his time between the Berkshires and northern California, is the author of the acclaimed novel *Ebb of the River.* Whistler's Inn has twelve guest rooms of varying sizes, each individually decorated, two with fireplaces. All have private baths. An extensive library, a living room, music room, sun porches and a large deck are available for guests' use. Six acres of grounds offer flowers, a sunken garden and peaceful seclusion. Cross-country ski and horseback riding trails start 200 yards from the house, seven downhill ski areas are within a 20-mile radius, lake beaches are nearby, and Tanglewood is only 1½ miles away. A continental breakfast, included in the rates, offers blueberry muffins, coffee or tea and orange juice. *5 Greenwood Street, Lenox, MA 01240; (413) 637-0975. Rates are expensive, lower off season. Well-supervised children are welcome. Open June 1 through October 31 and December 1 through March 20.*

Garden Gables Inn and Gift Shop. Mrs. Marie R. Veselik is the owner of Garden Gables, a very attractive establishment in Lenox, situated on lovely wooded grounds. The front part of the house was built around 200 years ago; the rest is about 70 years old. There are eight rooms for guests including four doubles with private baths, and two singles and two doubles each with running water, sharing two baths. Two furnished apartments are available. Guests are welcome to use the living room with fireplace and library, and outdoors are four acres of landscaped gardens that include a 72-foot-long swimming pool. There is a gift shop on the premises. Breakfast, at an extra charge, is served in the dining room. *141 Main Street, Lenox, MA 01240; (413) 637-0193. (Bottom of Church Hill, opposite St. Ann's Church.) Rates are moderate, higher in July and August. On weekends during those two months a minimum three-day stay is required, plus full payment in advance. No pets, please. Open all year.*

The Dalton House, Dalton, Massachusetts

Dalton House. The small town of Dalton is just to the east of Pittsfield, via Rtes. 9 and 8. Back in 1830, water from mountain streams turned some 350 waterwheels to power early industry in the area. The Dalton House was built in 1810 by T. D. Thompson, a Hessian soldier. Gary and Bernice Turetsky own the house nowadays, and offer guests a choice of nine rooms, all carpeted and heated, all with private baths. Each room has its own distinctive look; many are decorated with antiques and some have fireplaces. A large, wood-beamed, paneled lounge with fireplace, called The Loft Room, is available for guests' use. An attached greenhouse leads from the house to an old barn that has been converted into a flower and gift shop. For outdoor activities, an 18-hole golf course is within walking distance, as is horseback riding on beautiful country trails. All of the Berkshires' many offerings are easily accessible, including Tanglewood, Jacobs Pillow, the Shaker Village, Williamstown Summer Theatre, the Clark Institute, antique shops, excellent restaurants, fall foliage trips and skiing—both downhill and cross-country. A buffet breakfast is included in the rates: juice, English or blueberry muffins, jams and jellies, and coffee.

955 Main Street, Dalton, MA 01226; (413) 684-3854. Rates are moderate, lower off season. American Express, Visa and MasterCard are accepted. Children are welcome; no pets, please. Open all year.

The Northern Berkshires

THE WILLIAMSTOWN AREA AND MOHAWK TRAIL

The pretty, hilly Berkshire community of Williamstown was originally called West Hoosuck. In 1755, Colonel Ephraim Williams Jr., a regimental leader in the French and Indian War, willed his estate to the town. In return, he requested that the money be used to found a school—which later became Williams College—and that West Hoosuck be renamed Williamstown.

One of Williamstown's major lures is the splendid Sterling and Francine Clark Art Institute. An outstanding small art museum, the Clark displays more than thirty Renoirs as well as works of other famous Impressionists, paintings by Rembrandt, Rubens, Fragonard, Gainsborough and Winslow Homer, superb collections of old silver, and prints and drawings from the 15th to the 20th century. The Williamstown Summer Theatre Festival, held from late June to August, is considered one of the best in the country.

The curving Mohawk Trail, a section of Rte. 2, begins just east of Williamstown and ends about 38 miles east at Greenfield (or vice versa if you're traveling west). The drive traces part of the old trail used by the Indians of the Five Nations to pass between the Connecticut and Hudson River valleys. At the Hairpin Turn (which is exactly that), an observation tower provides sweeping views of northwestern Massachusetts and southern Vermont. Another scenic road in the region, off Rte. 2 just west of North Adams, leads you up Mount Greylock, Massachusetts' highest mountain at 3491 feet.

You will note a lot of signs in and around the area for the Natural Bridge. Formed millions of years ago, the marble arch spans a narrow gorge through which flows a stream. My personal recommendation is not to waste your money. New Hampshire, in particular, offers many more interesting and beautiful glacial gorges and rock formations, and I'd suggest you wait until you can explore *them*. The Bridge, by the way, is up for sale—for $280,000.

Victorian Tourist & Antique Home. President Woodrow Wilson's daughter once lived here, and Wilson paid a number of visits to the house while in office. The earliest part of the house was built in 1760 and remodelled in 1810; further restoration was made between 1916 and 1922 when the President's daughter was in residence. Today it belongs to Mary L. Dempsey, and is a lovely old place with nice porches and lots of trees and shrubbery. There are eight guest rooms, sharing three baths (one with shower, two with bathtub and shower). The rooms are all large and airy, furnished with antiques, and have TVs and radios. Guests may use the spacious living room with a fireplace. The house, which adjoins Williams College campus, is right next door to the Treadway Williams Inn and is within walking distance of several good restaurants and the Williamstown Summer Theatre. The Clark Art Institute is only ten minutes away.

1120 Main Street, Williamstown, MA 01267; (413) 458-3121. Rates are inexpensive. Children are welcome; pets are allowed except for large dogs. Open all year.

Green Mountain Guest House. Over in Greenfield, at the other end of the Mohawk Trail, there's a nice old guest house owned by Mrs. Florence V. Leach. Mrs. Leach, a delightful lady, is semi-retired and only takes in guests when she feels up to it—so please be sure and call ahead of time for a reservation. The Green Mountain Guest House, built in the 1850s, has four rooms for travelers including one twin, two doubles and one with two double beds. The last has a private bath; the others share a bath. The house is a small white structure with black shutters, set on landscaped grounds; the interior is furnished in family antiques, handmade braided rugs and Mrs. Leach's travel souvenirs. In summer, a large piazza is a pleasant place to sit. Nearby there is a municipal swimming area, a pretty spot formed in the Green River, and all manner of summer and winter sports are available in the region. Historic Deerfield, settled in the 1660s and twice destroyed in Indian massacres, is only a few miles away. No food is served at Green Mountain Guest House, but there are restaurants (and shops) within walking distance.

94 High Street (Rte. 2A), Greenfield, MA 01301; (413) 773-8748. (At corner of High and Maple Streets.) Rates are inexpensive to moderate. Well-behaved children are accepted, but please ask first; no pets. Please call or write in advance, to be sure rooms are available.

West of Boston

CONCORD

From the northern Berkshires you can follow Rte. 2 all the way east across the state to Concord, situated about 20 miles west of Boston. Just outside town, pick up Rte. 2A into Concord Center; it runs through the town and on to Lexington. From the southern Berkshires, take I-90 (the Massachusetts Turnpike) to Rte. 9 East at Framingham, then Rte. 126 north to Concord.

Guest Houses

Concord was incorporated in 1635. On April 19, 1775, the Minutemen of Concord and surrounding towns confronted the British redcoats at the North Bridge. That battle was the beginning of the American Revolution. The Minutemen won, forcing the British to march all the way back to Boston.

As you drive down Monument Street you'll see a parking lot on the right. Leave your car and walk across the road to the path leading to the North Bridge and the famous Minuteman statue. On the other side of the bridge you can walk up to the Minuteman National Historical Park Visitor's Center. It is in a beautiful mansion, built atop the hill with a superb view of the river below. In summer, the terraces below the house bloom with many varieties of lilies.

Visitors may also tour The Old Manse, beside the North Bridge. The house was built around 1765 for Rev. William Emerson; Ralph Waldo Emerson and Nathaniel Hawthorne both lived here for a time. Another Hawthorne house in Concord is The Wayside, on Lexington Road (Rte. 2A). Louisa May Alcott and her family resided, at different periods, in both The Wayside and the adjacent Orchard House. Both offer tours.

Don't miss the Hill Burying Ground (the oldest cemetery in Concord) on Lexington Road, a steep incline at Concord Center. The ancient, leaning, slate tombstones, topped with fearsome death's-heads, are engraved with fascinating legends and dire warnings. One of the most common, in one form or another, has this ghoulish message for passersby:

Stranger, stop and cast an eye—
As you are now, so once was I.
Death is a debt by nature due;
I've paid my debt and so must you.

Walden Pond, where Henry David Thoreau built his rustic cabin, is not far away—follow Walden Street across Rte. 2. A collection of Thoreau memorabilia may be seen at the Thoreau Lyceum on Belknap Street in Concord.

Concord is an absolutely delightful town for walking and sightseeing. There are many historic houses, museums and galleries to visit, and the Colonial Inn is an excellent place to dine, or to enjoy a drink in the old tavern room. The town is an ideal place to stay while you explore the area—from Lexington all the way into Boston. Another colorful place for dining is Longfellow's Wayside Inn in nearby Sudbury; it's the country's oldest continuously operating inn.

Hawthorne Inn. History buffs will surely enjoy a stay at this handsome old house in Concord, set among huge maple and pine trees just across the road from Hawthorne's Wayside and the Alcotts' Orchard House. The land on which it sits was owned by several of Concord's 19th-century greats, beginning with Ralph Waldo Emerson. He deeded the property to Bronson Alcott in 1844, when Alcott returned from his Fruitlands experiment. During the following ten years Alcott, with the help of his daughter Louisa and her sisters, grew fruit and vegetables on the land. He also built a bathhouse there, in what he considered to be the finest example of his own "Rustic Architecture." In 1855, Nathaniel Hawthorne purchased the property and planted a row of pine trees leading to the bathhouse. (Two of the trees are still standing.) Hawthorne sold the land to George A. Gray, who, in 1870, with his artist/genealogist son, built the house you see today.

Gregory Burch and Marilyn Mudry now own Hawthorne Inn and have five comfortable rooms for guests. Three full baths are shared; two rooms also have sinks. All are furnished with antiques, such as a mahogany Sheraton canopy bed, circa 1800, and several double brass beds. Handmade quilts add a homey touch to the rooms. Guests are invited to enjoy the Common Room with its old wood floor, Oriental carpet, fireplace and books. The bay-windowed room, accented by cinnamon-colored walls, offers more antique furniture including a marvelous Empire secretary. Throughout the house guests will note Greg Burch's own original art and sculpture, plus a fine collection of Japanese *ukiyo-e* block prints (circa 1780-1850). In addition, some 18th-century American pieces and pre-Columbian curios are on display.

A continental breakfast, served in the dining room, is included in the rates. Your hosts feature freshly-ground coffee, homebaked goods and fresh fruit—sometimes including their own raspberries, grown on the property.

462 Lexington Road (Rte. 2A), Concord, MA 01742; (617) 369-5610. Rates are expensive. Children are welcome; no pets, please. Ample parking is available. Open all year, except for the month of January.

OLD STURBRIDGE VILLAGE, QUABBIN RESERVOIR AND WARE

If you're heading east from the southern Berkshires via the Massachusetts Turnpike, about halfway across the state (between Springfield and Worcester) you'll see the sign for Old

Guest Houses

Sturbridge Village, at Exit 9. Located on Rte. 20, Old Sturbridge is a re-created village of the 1800s with a working farm and animals, a blacksmith's shop, pewterer, pottery, old houses, a tavern and much more. One shop makes delicious cookies using old-fashioned recipes; a long line of people is often outside, everyone happily sniffing the aroma of the warm, freshly-baked goodies. Plan to spend a full day at the Village—there's a lot to see.

The enormous Quabbin Reservoir, northwest of Old Sturbridge Village, is a lure for bird-watchers (the rare bald eagle nests here) and fishermen. There is excellent cross-country skiing in the winter, too. The Quabbin, formed by flooding five towns, is a beautiful area surrounded by pine forests; it has been described as a cross between the English Lake Country and the Scandinavian fiords.

In Ware, a small New England town ten minutes from Quabbin Reservoir and twenty miles northwest of Old Sturbridge Village, you'll find a charming, hospitable guest house that makes an ideal base for touring the region. Also, if you're going to or returning from Tanglewood in the Berkshires, the house is a fine halfway point at which to spend the night.

The Wildwood Inn. Margaret and Geoffrey Lobenstine, and twin daughters Heather and Lori, welcome guests to their comfortable old Victorian house, built in the 1880s. Travelers may choose from five rooms, each with its own distinctive character, sharing two baths. They're all designed to display the Lobenstines' collection of antique quilts and handmade afghans, and are named after them—the name embroidered in a small frame on the door. The Old Embroidery Quilt Master Guest Room, for example, features a lovely blue and white quilt, plus a four-poster bed and four-window bay. All of the beds have dual control electric blankets. Downstairs a large yet cozy country parlor is furnished mainly with American primitives including a cobbler's bench coffee table, spinning wheel and an unusual old pie safe. A magnificent "log cabin" quilt hangs on one wall, and a wooden carpenter's chest contains games and a variety of puzzles. There's an intriguing collection of books, too.

Weary travelers are often greeted with a cup of hot herbal tea. Breakfast, included in the rates, offers such good things as homemade applesauce bread, popovers or Peach Point muffins, accompanied by homemade peach butter, juice, coffee or tea. For a small extra charge, guests may indulge in special treats like Puff Pancakes, Lemon Twist or Chipmunk Pie— which does *not* include chipmunks! In afternoons or evenings, visitors are invited to sit beside the parlor's tiled fireplace and sip wine (BYOB) from the family's old pewter goblets, have a warming cup of cocoa, or toast marshmallows.

Wildwood Inn is set on two acres of wooded grounds edged by stone walls. Some of the fir trees, Mrs. Lobenstine confides, were illicitly smuggled (in the dark of night) out of the Quabbin Reservoir area before it was flooded. A grand old chestnut tree, one of the few remaining in the region, was purchased by a previous owner for twenty-five cents some 60 years ago. Directly behind the property are woods and a river, for hiking and canoeing—the Lobenstines have their own canoe. Tennis courts are nearby, and a short drive will bring you to a deliciously icy, brook-fed swimming hole. In winter ice skating and sledding are available.

121 Church Street, Ware, MA 01082; (413) 967-7798. (Take Exit 8 from the Massachusetts Turnpike; go left on Rte. 32 and follow to its end at Main Street in Ware. Bear right onto Main and go three traffic lights; bear left onto Church Street at the traffic light by the fountain. The house is ¾s of a mile on the right.) Rates are moderate. Older children are welcome, but please check first for small children. No pets, please. Open all year.

The North Shore

SALEM/MARBLEHEAD

The North Shore and Cape Ann may be reached from Boston via Rte. 1A; from west of Boston, take Rte. 128 north, then Rte. 114 east to Salem. Marblehead is further out on 114.

Salem's history is well known; in the witchcraft hysteria of 1692, 19 men and women were hanged for supposedly practicing "the diabolical arts." You can follow the whole intriguing story at the Salem Witch Museum, and explore the Witch House where Judge Jonathan Corwin held preliminary examinations of some of the accused witches.

The House of Seven Gables, setting for Nathaniel Hawthorne's novel, is also open to the public, as are a number of other 17th-century homes. Salem's sea-going past is on view at the Salem Maritime National Historic Site and in the superb Peabody Museum.

Guest Houses

Marblehead's snug harbor is one of the loveliest anywhere; the view from Fort Sewell is fantastic. One thing about Marblehead—prepare to get lost. Asking directions doesn't help much; the answers are too confusing. I have occasionally resorted to begging for help at the firehouse, and once even received a personal escort to my destination! But losing your way just adds to the fun; Marblehead is one of the most charming towns you will ever see. Its streets are very narrow, very steep and twisty, and totally enchanting.

The Suzannah Flint House/Bed & Breakfast. This wonderful old house in Salem was built around 1795 by Suzannah Flint, a widow. A number of other women owned the house over the years, and today Charlotte S. Post, also a widow, is your gracious hostess. Four very attractive air-conditioned rooms are available for guests, including two with twin beds and two with double beds, sharing one bath. The large second-floor bedroom, furnished in antiques, boasts a McIntyre mantel. Three of the bedrooms have working fireplaces, as do the upstairs sitting room and downstairs living room. Outdoors is a charming garden from which flowers, in season, are picked daily for each room. Mrs. Post serves her guests a breakfast of fresh fruit, homemade fruit breads and coffee, included in the rates. All of Salem's multitude of attractions are minutes away, including many fine restaurants and shops.
98 Essex Street, Salem, MA 01970; (617) 744-5281. Rates are moderate; group and weekly rates are available. Visa and MasterCard are accepted. There's parking at the house. Open all year, except possibly for a period in February or March.

The Daniels House. Mrs. Catherine B. Gill is the owner of the historic Daniels House in Salem. It was built in 1667 by Stephen Daniels, a sea captain, enlarged by his great-grandson in 1756, and remained in the Daniels family until 1931. In 1945, the house was converted into a comfortable guest house, furnished throughout with genuine antiques, including canopy beds and a marvelous assortment of Colonial items. There are four large, colorful rooms for guests, all with private baths. Visitors will especially enjoy the huge, walk-in fireplaces on the ground floor, complete with age-scarred old wooden mantels and brick hearths. To the rear of the house is a lovely shaded terrace, paved with bricks and stone, and bright with flowers and hanging baskets of greenery. It's a fine

Stephen Daniels House, Salem, Massachusetts

place to sit and relax in complete seclusion. Coffee and tea are offered at no charge; a full breakfast is available upon request for an extra charge. Salem's shops, restaurants, historic houses, museums and fascinating waterfront are all within walking distance. Beaches are nearby.

1 Daniels Street, Salem, MA 01970; (617) 744-5709. (At the corner of Essex and Daniels Streets, about three blocks from the Hawthorne Hotel in downtown Salem.) Rates are moderate. Children and pets are welcome. Space for two cars is available at house, more on street. Open all year.

The Coach House Inn. Captain E. Augustus Emmerton, builder of this elegant 19th-century home, was born in Salem in 1827; in later years he commanded the barque *Sophronia* and the ship *Neptune's Favorite*. A central figure in the development of the China Trade, Captain Emmerton sailed 'round the world to exotic places like Zanzibar and the Far East. Today, Stephen and Patricia Kessler own the old Coach House and have twelve comfortable rooms for guests, furnished in period style, most with private baths. The house is three-quarters of a mile from town, two blocks from a pleasant park with swimming pool, tennis courts and beaches. No food is served, but the Kesslers are planning a breakfast room for morning coffee and doughnuts.

284 Lafayette Street (Rtes. 114 and 1A), Salem, MA 01970; (617) 744-4092. Rates are moderate to expensive. American Express, Visa and MasterCard are accepted. Children are welcome; no pets, please. Parking is available. Open all year.

Guest Houses

Pleasant Manor Inn. A classic example of Victorian architecture, Pleasant Manor is located on Rte. 114 in Marblehead. Owners Richard and Takami Phelan have thirteen rooms for guests: six triples and two twins with private baths, and three triples and two doubles sharing baths. All are decorated with period furnishings, some with four-poster beds, and include coffee makers (plus supplies for same). A hall refrigerator is available for keeping perishables or cold drinks. There's a large sitting room with TV, and outdoors, a tennis court. The beach is only 1/8th of a mile away; restaurants and shops are within easy walking distance.

264 Pleasant Street (Rte. 114), Marblehead, MA 01945; (617) 631-5843. Rates are moderate, lower off season. Children and pets are welcome, but pets must not be left unattended in room. Off-street parking is available. Open all year.

Nautilus Guest House. Mrs. Ethel M. Dermody's Marblehead house is 178 years old, and furnished in period style. It is right across the road from the public landing and Marblehead Harbor where hundreds of impressive yachts moor all summer. Mrs. Dermody has owned the Nautilus for almost twenty years; many of her guests return year after year. She has eight rooms sharing three baths in summer, four rooms in winter. No food is served, but many restaurants are within walking distance. Mrs. Dermody especially recommends a small place across the street; it opens at 5:30 a.m. to accommodate the town's fishermen, and is very reasonable.

68 Front Street, Marblehead, MA 01945; (617) 631-1703. Rates are moderate. Children are welcome; no pets, please. Open all year.

GLOUCESTER/ROCKPORT

From Salem, follow Rte. 1A north to Beverly and pick up Rte. 127 and then 127A north; it is a particularly scenic drive through pretty towns and out along Cape Ann.

Before you reach the fishing port of Gloucester, you might wish to pay a visit to Hammond Castle, five miles southwest. It's on Hesperus Avenue (the shore road), two miles south of Rte. 127. Inventor John Hays Hammond built it to house his collection of rare art objects. It looks like a medieval castle, and is full of fascinating items like authentic medieval facades surrounding an indoor pool. A special device changes the weather in this room, from sun to rain to moonlight. Concerts are given year-round on an 8000-pipe organ in the Great Hall. Mr. Hammond had a wicked sense of humor, apparently. He once rigged a boat, painted black, with remote control and—from his dining room, ran it around the coastal area, terrifying local fishermen and boaters.

Down at the harbor in Gloucester you will probably want to take a picture of the famous statue, "The Gloucester Fisherman," a memorial to fishermen lost at sea. Prowl around some of the wharves—they smell just as fishy today as they did in the days of *Captains Courageous*. Each year around the end of June there is a four-day fishermen's celebration called St. Peter's Fiesta, with parades, fireworks and the Blessing of the Fleet. Children will like the Gloucester Fishermen's Museum, at Rogers and Porter Streets. Kids are invited to touch and operate the exhibits, listen to foghorns, and watch films. Real live fishermen come to talk to the youngsters, show them how to mend nets, and even take them on tours down to the wharves.

Rockport is an artists' colony, and art galleries are everywhere. Bearskin Neck, a tiny street off Dock Square, is lined with quaint little shops and restaurants, absolutely packed with tourists in the summertime. In the early 1800s, Rockport had a flourishing granite industry. Huge blocks of granite were hauled by oxen from the quarries to the harbor. Most of the old, abandoned quarries are on private land today, but you can glimpse one or two from the road just past the bridge at Pigeon Cove.

Shortly beyond Pigeon Cove is the turnoff to Halibut Point, the northernmost tip of Cape Ann. It's not easy to find, as it is not always marked. Ask someone for directions. A long, woodsy path will take you out to the Point, a marvelous place of tumbled granite rocks and crashing ocean surf.

Colonial Guest House and Gift Shop. Robert and Barbara Balestraci's guest house in East Gloucester is of Colonial architecture, as you might have guessed. It was built more than 100 years ago and is very handsome indeed. The Balestracis have seven guest rooms, all large and with private baths. Some rooms have double beds, others a double bed plus trundle (which sleeps two) or a queen-size bed. Outside, there is a lovely tree-shaded lawn with a great view of Gloucester Harbor, and plenty of chairs to sit in while you watch. Guests may use the barbecue pit and picnic table, too. The house is a few minutes' walk from an excellent beach, and boats may be rented practically on the property. Restaurants and shops —antique and other varieties—and the Rocky Neck Art Colony are all close by. A continental breakfast is included in the rates.

28 Eastern Point Road, East Gloucester, MA 01930; (617) 281-1953. (Between Niles and Rocky Neck: from Rte. 127 follow Western Ave., Rogers Street, Main Street, then East Main Street to lights; bear right up hill on East Main.) Rates are moderate. Children are welcome; no pets, please. Open all year.

The Inn on Cove Hill. A charming bed and breakfast establishment, this classic Federal house is located right in the heart of Rockport, within easy walking distance of restaurants, shops, galleries and the harbor. The house is white with black shutters, with an exceptionally handsome doorway. Inside, architectural connoisseurs will delight in the Christian cross doors with "H" and "L" hinges, carefully preserved wainscoting and dentil molding, and wide pumpkin pine floors. There's a fine ceramic tile fireplace and a graceful spiral staircase—built with thirteen steps, a common tribute to the original thirteen colonies.

Owners John and Marjorie Pratt have ten rooms for guests: four with one double and one twin bed and six with one double bed. Seven of the rooms have private baths; three share a hall bath. The rooms, with TVs, are decorated with maple Colonial furniture and cricket chairs; the color schemes are based on predominant shades in the pretty print and floral wallpapers. Personal touches are everywhere: handmade pin cushions for emergency mending, handmade afghans and quilts for nippy nights, vases of daisies in summer, pumpkins in autumn.

A third floor porch offers a panoramic view of picturesque Rockport Harbor and the ocean beyond; whales may sometimes be sighted during migration. Guests may also use the attractive living room, furnished in a blend of new and antique pieces, the latter including a cherry Winthrop desk and Windsor chair built by a family ancestor some 150 years ago. A well-stocked bookcase provides magazines and works by Longfellow, Dickens and other classic authors. In the service room, guests may store snacks in the refrigerator or obtain ice buckets and cubes. An information table with maps and lists of local events is another thoughtful touch. Outdoors, guests may relax at umbrella tables set around a hand-operated (and working) water pump set atop an enormous granite capstone, surrounded by masses of yellow Marguerite daisies.

The Pratts offer their guests a continental breakfast, included in the rates, served outside on the lawn in summer or brought on a tray to your room in winter. Breakfast consists of freshly-ground coffee, orange juice and homemade muffins—blueberry, cranberry, blackberry or pumpkin, depending on the season—elegantly served on lovely Royal Doulton and Wedgwood English bone china. Your hosts bake each morning, just so guests may wake up to the delicious aroma of hot muffins!

37 Mt. Pleasant Street, Rockport, MA 01966; (617) 546-2701. (Follow Rte. 127 into Rockport, then 127A to the house.) Rates are moderate. Children over 10 are welcome; no pets, please. Parking is available. Open all year.

The Seafarer. This pleasant house by the sea, built in the 1890s, has been welcoming guests continuously since 1900; it was once part of a larger inn complex. Located in a tiny cove in Rockport, the Seafarer is surrounded on three sides by the ocean. A large veranda offers a grand view of the rocks and sea, and each of the seven guest rooms overlooks the ocean. All but one room have private baths. Instead of numbers on the doors, the rooms have authentic nautical brass plates designating quarters: Captain's, First Mate's, Master's and the like. Paintings by local artists are hung throughout the house. Guests are invited to enjoy the living room with fireplace and stereo; TV is available on request. Your hosts, Gerry and Mary Pepin, feel that their house offers a homelike, friendly atmosphere where guests may relax and enjoy the natural beauty of the sea. Juice and coffee are provided on the porch each morning, included in the rates. The Seafarer is a short walk from the village along paths that follow the ocean. Swimming beaches are nearby, too.

86 Marmion Way, Rockport, MA 01966; (617) 546-6248. Rates are moderate, lower off season. Children are welcome; no pets, please. Parking is available. Open April through November.

Ryan's House. It's a little house, and charming . . . of salt box architecture with natural shingles, set behind a white picket fence. Thick shrubbery and nice old shade trees are all around; there are a patio for cookouts and a lawn for sunbathing. Mrs. Anna Ryan has two rooms for guests, each with private bath, air conditioning, refrigerator and TV. The house is a five-minute walk from the village, and ten minutes from two beaches. It is on a quiet street, away from traffic, and features an art gallery on the premises.

1 Norwood Avenue, Rockport, MA 01966; (617) 546-6004. (Two blocks from center of town.) Rates are moderate. Ample parking is available. Open Memorial Day through Labor Day.

Lantana Guest House. Jack and Lempi Reed welcome guests to their comfortable old house, right in the center of Rockport. The eight guest rooms are all twin-bedded, most with private bath. For relaxing, try the living room and—out front—a spacious sundeck adorned with hanging pots of flowering lantanas. No food is served, but a number of fine restaurants are within a few minutes' walk.

22 Broadway, Rockport, MA 01966; (617) 546-3535. Rates are inexpensive to moderate, lower off season. Parking is available on premises. Open all year.

NEWBURYPORT

Newburyport still has the feeling and flavor of Colonial America. And High Street, with its collection of 17th-century and Federalist houses, is practically a museum of magnificent architecture. Shipowners and sea captains built many of the homes back when the town was a bustling seaport. The U.S. Coast Guard started here, too. Signs with the hull of a clipper ship mark the Clipper Trail, a walking tour that will lead you to many of Newburyport's places of interest. Excellent restaurants and shops of all kinds are located in the restored area along the waterfront.

Plum Island, a few miles from town, is the site of the Parker River National Wildlife Refuge, with miles of sand dunes and beaches. It's great for hiking, picnicking, bird-watching, and —in winter—cross-country skiing.

Newburyport is 38 miles north of Boston and 17 miles south of Portsmouth, New Hampshire. To reach it from Rockport, follow Rte. 127 around Cape Ann, then pick up Rte. 133 west to Ipswich, then 1A north. Crane's Beach, one of the finest on the Atlantic coast, is a short drive from Ipswich. From Boston, take Rte. 1 north to I-95 and follow I-95 north to Rte. 113; go east to Newburyport.

Morrill Place. Newburyport reached its peak of prosperity as a commercial and shipping center in the late 1700s and early 1800s; trade with Europe and China made it the seventh largest port in the nation. It was during that period that many of the town's most beautiful homes were constructed. The Morrill mansion, one of Newburyport's finest, was built in 1806 by Captain William Hoyt. In 1836, Henry W. Kinsman, a junior law partner of Daniel Webster's, bought the place . . . and Mr. Webster was a frequent visitor. Gayden Morrill, mayor of Newburyport, purchased the house in 1897; the Morrill family retained ownership for 84 years.

Mrs. Rose Ann Hunter, who previously owned the Benjamin Choate House in Newburyport, took possession of Morrill Place in 1979, opening it to guests. An elegant three-story Federal edifice, the 22-room house includes 12 fireplaces and 93 windows, as well as a host of fine architectural features such as lovely cornices, mantels, balustrades and a graceful hanging staircase. There are ten guest bedrooms, sharing five baths. All of the rooms are furnished in antiques: one offers a queen-size canopy four-poster and another a three-quarter Jenny Lind bed. Guests are invited to use the summer and winter porches (the latter with TV), the formal front parlor and library. There's a rooftop widow's walk, too. The restored historic area, with scores of shops and restaurants and many of Newburyport's other marvelous old houses, is only a five-minute walk away. Plum Island and superb beaches are five minutes away by car.

Mrs. Hunter serves her guests a continental breakfast of juice, coffee and baked goods or English muffins with jam, and afternoon tea, all included in the rates. For Newburyport visitors unable to stay at the house there are daily tours at 3 p.m. A nominal fee is charged, and the tour is followed by tea —served hot during the winter in the library by the fire, or iced in the summer on the porch or terrace.

209 High Street, Newburyport, MA 01950; (617) 462-2808. (From I-95, exactly two miles on High Street.) Rates are moderate. Well-behaved children and pets are welcome. Parking is available at the house. Open all year.

Benjamin Choate House. Another of Newburyport's dignified Federal houses, this handsome structure was built in 1794 by Benjamin Choate, a shipbuilder and educator. Herbert A. Fox now owns the house, and has five rooms available for guests. They include two doubles with private baths, one twin, one double with working fireplace, and one single (the last three sharing a full bath and powder room). The rooms are elegantly decorated with period furniture, Oriental rugs, original Old Master prints from Mr. Fox's private collection, and fine limited edition graphics printed at Fox's Boston lithography shop, where he is a Master Printer.

Guests are invited to relax by the fireplace in the beautiful front parlor with its graceful Empire couch, floor-length satin drapes and exquisite hand-colored Japanese woodcuts. The Choate House offers a continental breakfast of homemade muffins and coffee or tea, included in the rates. Breakfast is served in the comfortable old kitchen—a set of early 19th-century porcelain canisters over the massive fireplace and great-grandmother's handmade lace tablecloth completing the old-fashioned charm of the room.

25 Tyng Street, Newburyport, MA 01950; (617) 423-2559. (Four miles from I-95, one mile from Rte. 1A and Rte. 1.) Rates are moderate. Visa and MasterCard are accepted. Quiet, well-behaved children and pets are welcome. Parking is available. Open all year.

The South Shore and Cape Cod

From Boston, the most direct routes to Cape Cod are I-93 and then 3 south. Along the way you'll see signs for historic Plymouth, over on Rte. 3A. After you cross the Sagamore Bridge on Rte. 3 over the Cape Cod Canal, Rte. 6 east (the Mid-Cape Highway) will take you directly to Provincetown. An alternate, more scenic, way to explore the region is to make a circle trip. From the Sagamore Bridge head south to Rte. 28 and down to Bourne, Falmouth and Woods Hole.

Then take Rte. 28 east along the Cape's southern shore and north to Orleans where you pick up Rte. 6 to Provincetown. To return, follow Rte. 6A west along the northern shore.

PLYMOUTH
The first American settlement north of Jamestown, Virginia, Plymouth was founded by the Pilgrims in 1620. A replica of the original *Mayflower* is moored in the harbor and may be toured. The ship is amazingly tiny, only 90 feet long. Pilgrim Village and Plimoth Plantation (the latter is three miles away) both show visitors what life was like in the 1600s. And of course, Plymouth Rock is located here, too. It might well be called Plymouth Pebble, as it is not exactly as impressive as most people expect. But it is symbolic, and certainly something everyone wants to see.

Colonial House Inn. Located just south of the center of Plymouth, this nice old Colonial wood frame house was built around 1860. Owners Oscar and Olga Isaacs have six rooms for guests including doubles and triples, with private baths. Guests may also use the comfortable living room. No food is served; restaurants, shops, Plymouth's historic sites and beaches are one mile away.
207 Sandwich Street (Rte. 3A), Plymouth, MA 02360; (617) 746-2087. (One mile south of Plymouth Center.) Rates are moderate, lower off season. Children are welcome; no pets, please. Open April–November.

BOURNE/FALMOUTH/WOODS HOLE
Monument Beach at Bourne offers great swimming, and the Aptucxet Trading Post, a re-creation of a 1627 Pilgrim-Dutch trading post, is fun to explore. Falmouth is an exceptionally pretty Cape town, with lots of trees, a nice village green and many old houses. Old Silver Beach is one of the finest on the Cape with clean, soft sand and fairly warm water. Woods Hole, down at the bottom of the Cape, is the home of the famed Woods Hole Oceanographic Institution. Ferries for Martha's Vineyard and Nantucket leave from Woods Hole, and cruises to Martha's Vineyard are available from Falmouth.

Bay Breeze Guest House. Located right on Buzzards Bay at Monument Beach, Joe Rogers' 75-year-old guest house is a relaxing, informal place to stay. A large porch with comfortable wicker chairs overlooks the bay, and a semi-private beach is directly in front. Guests may use the nearby public tennis courts. All seven guest rooms have ocean views, and share three baths. No meals are served, but a large kitchen and dining room are available for a small fee. Guests are also welcome to enjoy the well-stocked library and TV lounge. All manner of restaurants are nearby.

Shore Road, P.O. Box 307, Monument Beach, Cape Cod, MA 02553; (617) 759-5069. (Just outside of Bourne.) Rates are inexpensive. Children are welcome; no pets, please. Open April through September.

Elm Arch Inn. Mr. and Mrs. Harry C. Richardson are your hosts at this historic Colonial guest house in Falmouth. Built in 1810 as the private residence of Captain Silas Jones, the house was bombarded by the British frigate *Nimrod* on January 28, 1814. The wall in the dining room still carries the cannonball scar. Since 1926, three generations of the Richardson family have owned and operated Elm Arch Inn. There are 24 rooms (in two buildings) for guests. Twelve have private baths; the rest share three baths. The rooms, attractively decorated in Colonial style, feature antiques and reproductions, braided rugs and patchwork quilts. Some offer four-poster canopy beds. Several living rooms, a TV room, large screened-in porch and a swimming pool are also available for guests' use. In season, complimentary coffee is served. Elm Arch is within walking distance of Falmouth's restaurants, shops and the beach.

Elm Arch Way, Falmouth, MA 02540; (617) 548-0133. (Off Main Street, two blocks east of the new Town Hall.) Rates are moderate, lower off season. Children are welcome; pets are allowed during the winter months. Ample parking is available. Open all year.

Mostly Hall, Bed & Breakfast. Even though situated on Falmouth's main street just across from the village green, Mostly Hall is almost invisible to passersby. The house, surrounded by thick shrubbery, is well back from the road behind an impressive wrought iron fence. But if you peer carefully through the trees, you'll see a most unusual structure. In this region of gray-shingled Cape Cod cottages and traditional sea captains' Federal or Victorian homes, this striking mansion is virtually unique. It is a classic example of Southern architecture, a typical New Orleans Garden District home.

Mostly Hall, Falmouth, Massachusetts

Virginia Austin, who owns Mostly Hall with her husband Jim and their daughter, tells the tale of how such a house came to be constructed so far away from its native setting. In 1849, a Yankee sea captain named Nye planned to bring his New Orleans bride to Falmouth. She, however, announced that she would not come North unless he built a house similar to her own home. He did, and the result is this spacious edifice with high ceilings, airy rooms, long, narrow windows with louvered shutters, and an exterior gallery extending all the way around the house. The living quarters are, in Southern fashion, set up off the ground on posts; the original kitchen and servants' quarters were on the ground floor/basement level. High at the top of the structure is a widow's walk—probably Captain Nye's personal addition.

The name "Mostly Hall," by the way, was given the place at a much later date. When the previous owners moved in, their young son—after glimpsing the expansive entranceway—cried: "Wow, it's mostly hall!"

The hospitable Austins, who opened the house to guests in 1980, have three attractively-decorated double rooms for visitors, all with private baths. Upstairs, via a deep gold-carpeted stairway, are the Wicker Room and French Room, the latter boasting two antique sleigh beds. The stairs, incidentally, are long and steep and some guests may prefer to stay in the Canopy Room on the first floor, just off the central hallway. It offers a fine four-poster canopy bed with a colorful patchwork quilt. Sometime in the future the Austins plan to add three more guest rooms and a carriage house apartment.

Guest Houses

Guests are invited to use the large, elegant living room with its 14-foot ceilings, the woodwork done in Williamsburg blue. A full breakfast, included in the rates, is served in season at a dining table at the far end of the room. Ginny Austin arises early every morning to prepare homemade breads, rolls, crepes and quiches for her guests. Fresh fruit, juice and coffee or tea round out the repast, which may sometimes include Welsh rabbit served on English muffins with bacon, or eggs Benedict.

Outdoors, in addition to relaxing on the porch, guests have access to the lawn behind the house with flowers and many trees. (One of these days Jim and Ginny intend to build a gazebo for the lawn.) Indoors or out, Mostly Hall is a quiet, secluded haven, yet the house is only a minute's walk from Falmouth's many shops and restaurants.

27 Main Street, Falmouth, MA 02540; (617) 548-3786. (Opposite the Village Green.) Rates are moderate. No children under 16; no pets, please. Open May 15–November 15.

Sea Gull Lodge. This is a pretty house with a homelike air, also located in Falmouth. John and Doris Gouliamas have eight rooms for guests, sharing four baths. They have owned the Lodge since 1953, and some of their unusual Swedish antiques decorate the rooms. A living room with TV is for guests' use; outside are a patio and large yard. No food is served, but the house is close to restaurants, shops and the like.

41 Belvidere Road, P.O. Box 564, Falmouth, MA 02540; (617) 548-0679. (Follow Rte. 28 east in Falmouth; turn right on Scranton Avenue and then right on Lowry Road to Belvidere.) Rates are inexpensive. Children are welcome; no pets, please. Open all year.

Vineyard View Lodge. Dick and Gloria Faulkner own Vineyard View in Falmouth, a family-type house with a swimming pool and patio in the backyard. It's on a quiet street, safe for children, with a park area in front for kids to play in. The ocean is two blocks away. The five large, airy guest rooms all have private baths and twin beds. There's a living room with TV, and outdoors, a patio with barbecue grill. The house is within walking distance of restaurants, shops and various activities. The Faulkners really welcome families with children over seven. No food is served but they will get you going in the morning with hot coffee. They also provide free transportation to or from the bus station or Hyannis airport, and will drive you to the *Island Queen* ferry (three blocks away) that sails to Martha's Vineyard.

10 Worcester Court West, Falmouth, MA 02540; (617) 548-2364. (Five blocks south of intersection of Jones Road and Rte. 28.) Rates are moderate. Open June 15–Labor Day.

The Gladstone Inn. Built in the late 1800s, the oceanfront Gladstone Inn in Falmouth has been taking in guests for around 80 years. Jim and Gayle Carroll are your friendly hosts at the very comfortable house, restored by Jim, a retired Air Force officer. They have nine bedrooms for guests, three singles and six doubles. Four baths are shared; every room has a sink. Most of the rooms have views of the ocean and Martha's Vineyard. The spacious sun porch, overlooking the ocean, offers plenty of chairs and tables, TV, and refrigerators for keeping perishables. Beaches, swimming, golfing, sailing and biking are easily accessible, as are restaurants and shops. The Carrolls serve their guests a continental breakfast, with homemade jam, included in the rates.

219 Grand Avenue S., Falmouth, MA 02540; (617) 548-9851. (At the corner of Grand Avenue and Montgomery, on the beach in Falmouth Heights.) Rates are moderate. Children and pets are welcome, but not encouraged. Open May 15–October 15.

Schofields' Guest House. Clyde E. Schofield's large century-old white house is right on the ocean in Falmouth Heights. He has twelve carpeted bedrooms for guests, sharing six baths, and two broad porches for relaxing (plus a sundeck for tanning or boat-watching). No food is served; a few minutes' walk will take you to Falmouth's many restaurants and shops.

335 Grand Avenue S., Falmouth, MA 02540; (617) 548-4648. (Take Rte. 28 through Falmouth Center, then Falmouth Heights Road to the waterfront. Follow shore road to corner of Grand Avenue S. and Great Hill Avenue.) Rates are moderate. Children are welcome. Open all year.

The Marlborough. A charming "full Cape" house set on a wooded half acre in Woods Hole, the Marlborough is owned by Patricia Morris. There are four bedrooms for guests in the main house, plus a separate "gazebo-type" cottage. The rooms, which share a bath, are individually decorated with wicker, brass, iron and old wood antiques; the comfortable beds are covered with colorful custom or handcrafted quilts and spreads. The cottage, ideal for honeymooners, has its own bath and screened-in porch. Guests may use the paddle tennis court, barbecuing and picnic facilities, play croquet or enjoy a restful hour reclining in a hammock. About a mile away are the ferries to Martha's Vineyard and Nantucket, a private beach (with lifeguard on duty), the Woods Hole Aquarium, and nature walks on Quisset campus. A 3½-mile bike path runs from Woods Hole to Falmouth. Guests at The Marlborough are served a continental breakfast, included in the rates, consisting of coffee, juice or fruit, and hot, homebaked breads such as banana, zucchini, brioche or scones. (Your hostess says that one can stay for a week and not have the same bread twice!)

320 Woods Hole Road, Woods Hole, MA 02543; (617) 548-6218. (Follow Rte. 28 south to Woods Hole.) Rates are moderate, lower off season. Older children are welcome; no babies or pets, please. Open all year.

HYANNIS/CHATHAM

Rte. 28 takes you east to Hyannis; if you are traveling on Rte. 6, however, take the Rte. 132 exit into town. Hyannis is a well-populated community, very busy in summer. Its large number of shops and restaurants are a big draw, especially on rainy days. The commercial aspects of the town appeal to many travelers; others vastly prefer to seek out areas which offer more of the authentic charm of Cape Cod. The famed "Kennedy Compound" is in nearby Hyannisport, but none of the houses are open to the public. Boats leave from Hyannis for Martha's Vineyard and Nantucket in summer, fall and spring.

Further along Rte. 28 you will come to Chatham, right at the southeast corner of the Cape, on the "elbow." It is one of the older townships, settled in 1656 by a handful of Pilgrims, and one of the nicest. In and around the village you'll find a wide range of posh shops and good restaurants. At the Chatham Fish Pier, visitors may watch the small fishing fleet unload its catch daily after 2 p.m. And a marvelous wilderness area is just offshore—the Monomoy National Wildlife Refuge.

The Yellow Door Guest House. A brown-shingled Cape Cod house, the Yellow Door in Hyannis is owned by Margaret A. Goodman. It is a comfortable place, with a nice sundeck and yard for sitting. Five rooms are available for guests, one with private bath; the others share two baths. Guests are welcome to use the large living room with TV. The house is close to just about everything in town, and the rates are a real bargain, especially for the Cape.

6 Main Street, Hyannis, MA 02601; (617) 775-0321. Rates are inexpensive. Children and pets are welcome. There's ample parking. Open all year.

The Olson Home. Axel and Reliance Olson run this small guest house in Chatham, offering friendly, native Cape Cod hospitality. Theirs is a modern Cape-type house in a quiet area, furnished with both contemporary and antique furniture. There is a nice porch to sit on and guests have their own private entrance. Oyster Pond, only two minutes away, usually provides a cool breeze. The Olsons have one large guest room with twin beds, a large closet, and private bath with tub and shower. It is really a suite, as a small living room goes with it. No food is served, but restaurants are only a couple of minutes away.

26 Stage Harbor Road, Chatham, MA 02633; (617) 945-9233. (Turn at rotary in center of town.) Rates are moderate, lower off season. Open May–late fall.

The Moorings. The Moorings, located on Main Street in Chatham, was originally the estate of Rear Admiral Charles Rockwell, U.S.N. Rockwell and his wife Mary built the house in 1865; in 1908 the Admiral retired from the Navy to spend the rest of his years there. A blend of stately Victorian and traditional Cape Cod architecture, the house includes such distinctive features as two-story bay windows, designed as the Admiral's observation post, and the attached flower-surrounded gazebo. Today, Jan and Earl Rush own The Moorings. Although it's termed a "motor inn" and does have a small motel unit out back, the central structure of The Moorings is Admiral Rockwell's grand old home. The house offers five rooms for travelers, all with private baths. They include twins, doubles and one king, and are decorated in appropriate Victorian style. The large Admiral's Room is especially impressive with a red velvet king-sized bed and carved scallop-shell fireplace. Guests are invited to enjoy the elegant wood-paneled parlor with player piano and fireplace, the latter boasting a handsomely carved floor-to-ceiling mantel. No food is served except in stormy weather, when a complimentary continental breakfast is provided.

Guest Houses

In addition to the guest house, accommodations for longer stays are available in the old restored Coach House which has four semi-private rooms, and the attached Colonial-style motel with four private rooms. There are also several efficiency units and a two-bedroom cottage on the grounds. The Chatham Light is less than a five-minute walk away, as are beaches and boating. Tennis, golf, fishing, restaurants and shops are easily accessible, and The Moorings has bicycles (including tandem) for guests to use at no charge.

326 Main Street, Chatham, MA 02633; (617) 945-0848. Rates are moderate to expensive, lower off season. American Express, Visa and MasterCard are accepted. Children are welcome (cribs available for babies); no pets, please. The guest house is open all year; the Coach House, motel, efficiencies and cottage are open April through October.

The Calico Cat Guest House and Gift Shop. This striking edifice, also located on Chatham's Main Street—just beyond the village—includes two very different styles of architecture. Captain John Hallett built the older part, a "half Cape," in the late 1700s. The gleaming white Greek Revival addition was constructed in 1840 as a shop specializing in calico goods. The shop still sells calico items today (aprons, potholders, stuffed animals and cloth) plus gifts of handcrafted wood, stoneware, brass and iron, country candy, and a great deal more. For travelers, Mrs. Beatrice Zaremba has four rooms above the shop including three doubles and one single, one with private bath. She does not serve food, but an excellent restaurant is right next door and many others are in the area. Outdoors, a pleasant side lawn is a nice, shady place to sit.

193 Main Street, Chatham, MA 02633; (617) 945-1192. (In the old village, near the Chatham Light.) Rates are inexpensive. Children are welcome; no pets, please. Open mid-June–just after Labor Day.

PROVINCETOWN

Provincetown, way out at the very tip of Cape Cod, has a unique sort of charm, a mixture of Colonial New England seaport ambiance and contemporary tourism—spiced with a Portuguese flavor. It is a quaint, colorful town with a raft of tiny, winding byways running between the two major thoroughfares, Commercial and Bradford streets. Looming above is the imposing granite Pilgrim Monument, which visitors can climb for a sweeping view of the entire Cape. With lots of restaurants (a few offer excellent Portuguese food) and many distinctive shops and art galleries—Provincetown is fun to walk around. In fact, you may want to come without your car as parking is scarce. You can reach the area by bus, air, and even boat: a cruise ship makes the trip from Boston daily in season.

The Cape Cod National Seashore extends for miles along the coast, for bicycling, horseback riding, dune-buggy rides, fishing, swimming and beachcombing. Several visitor centers offer information on a host of walks and trails, house and lighthouse tours, and a variety of special programs including park ranger talks on Cape Cod history. Whale-watching excursions sail several times daily from Provincetown harbor. The voyages last about five hours, and humpback, finback and minke whales are regularly spotted—an awesome and unforgettable sight.

The Provincetown area and the two small villages of Truro and North Truro not far away are pretty much isolated from the rest of the Cape; the visitor can find blissful solitude along the beaches or the miles of rolling dunes and moors. It's a wild, barren region, very different and totally enchanting. Provincetown itself, however, can be a bit of a shock to visitors expecting a tranquil New England village, particularly at the height of the season. Then, the modern world collides with the town's 17th-century past—not to everyone's taste. The restaurants, bars, galleries and shops along narrow, one-way Commercial Street are mobbed with vacationers of every sort, including hordes of day-trippers and a large gay element. During the summer months the gay culture predominates, and is very visible, sometimes flamboyantly so. You will have to decide for yourself whether or not you will appreciate the scene—or would rather come in fall, winter or early spring when the town is quieter. The summer season is, also, a very busy one; visitors are advised to make reservations well in advance.

Provincetown has a wealth of handsome old houses, many dating from the 1700s and early 1800s. A large number of these, including some of the finest, are now guest houses. A few restrict clientele to only gay visitors; most welcome both straight and gay guests. Generally the two blend very well, and thoroughly enjoy the experience. If you feel you must know ahead of time which is which, just ask the proprietors. They will give an honest answer. Once you've arrived, they will also suggest which restaurants and bars to visit, to avoid experiencing culture shock.

151

Guest Houses

Asheton House. Of all the guest houses in Provincetown, this is perhaps the most elegant and beautifully furnished, down to the last perfect detail. Originally a whaling captain's home built around 1840, Asheton House is now owned by Jim Bayard and Les Schaufler. The house stands behind a Nantucket-style white fence; a graceful double set of steps leads up to the front door. From the lovely gardens and brick walks you can watch the fishing boats rounding Long Point. Guests may relax in the semi-formal English boxwood garden under rare Japanese Temple trees, or on the sheltered terrace in the rear. And your hosts provide an "eye-opener" of juice, coffee or tea each morning, included in the rates.

Asheton House has three guest rooms, all spacious and airy, appointed with antiques from the owners' private collection. One is a suite consisting of a bed/sitting room with French furnishings, a dressing room with wardrobe wall, a fireplace and private bath. The other two, equally attractive, share a bath. The Captain's Room, with American antiques, includes a queen-size 19th-century four-poster bed; the Safari Room, with two double beds, is furnished in natural wicker and bamboo and handsome campaign chests.

In addition, a charming early 1800s Cape house on the adjoining property offers four more guest rooms, sharing baths, and a three-room apartment. Each is individually decorated. The double-bed Deck Room with Oriental accessories and the double-bed Bay Room (with Chinese Chippendale arm chairs and a planter's chaise) both overlook the bay. The Lattice Room features wallpaper of white lattice on a brown background; the Paisley Room is American antique with a documentary pattern framing walls and ceiling; both have double beds.

3 Cook Street, Provincetown, MA 02657; (617) 487-9966. Rates are moderate to expensive, lower by the week and in fall, winter and spring. Parking is available; if you come by plane your hosts will meet you at the airport. Open all year.

Wave's Landing Guest House. Mrs. Dorothy Nearen operates Wave's Landing, a white house with black shutters. In summer windowboxes bloom with bright geraniums and petunias, and the picket fence out front is covered with roses. Inside, the house is typical Cape Cod-style with nine guest rooms, all spotless and comfortable, and a nice, friendly atmosphere. There are five baths, some private and some shared. Several studios for one or two persons are also available, by the week. Guests may use two pleasant lounges, both offering easy chairs, magazines and lots of plants. One of Wave's Landing's rooms (we're not telling which) may have a ghost! Your hostess reports that a guest telephoned her, after returning home from a week's stay at the house, and asked if anyone had ever mentioned seeing the figure of a woman in her room. Mrs. Nearen asked what she had been smoking; the guest laughed —but was quite sincere. No one else has ever seen the apparition, at least to date.

158 Bradford Street, Provincetown, MA 02657; (617) 487-9665 or 9198. (Corner of Pearl Street.) Rates are inexpensive to moderate. No children or pets, please. Some parking is available. Open Memorial Day weekend –Labor Day.

Bradford Gardens Inn. James Logan welcomes guests to this interesting old house, built in 1820. Furnished in antiques, with original paintings on the walls, Bradford Gardens has seven working fireplaces. Accommodations include five double rooms and three suites, all charmingly varied in character, and all with private baths and color TV. The Chimney Nook, for instance, offers water and garden views and an old fireplace nook; the Sun Gallery Suite, with private entrance, also has a fireplace and garden view. A full country breakfast is included in the rates, served in winter in the Morning Room with its central fireplace and large bay window overlooking the garden. In spring and summer, breakfast is served in the beautifully landscaped gardens among flowering fruit trees and rose bushes; in May the splendid Japanese cherry bursts into bloom. Behind the main house is the Loft Lodge, a stunningly magnificent structure with two loft bedrooms, a cathedral-ceilinged living room, a gigantic fireplace, deck, patio and complete kitchen. Frederick Waugh, the renowned Marine artist, built the lodge as his studio around 1925 out of ships' ribs, knees and timbers hauled from old wrecks. Hans Hofmann, an abstract expressionist, purchased the studio in 1945; he painted and taught there for some twenty years.

178 Bradford Street, Provincetown, MA 02657; (617) 487-1616. Rates are expensive. American Express, Visa and MasterCard are accepted. Families with children under 12 are welcome, but will be given outside suites only. No pets, please. Parking is available. Open April 1 –December 1.

Guest Houses

The Joshua Paine House. Albert and Marie Smith feel that their house is one of the most charming in Provincetown. It is furnished in antiques, including some very old handmade quilts; guests enjoy seeing the unusual circular cellar. A white picket fence in front is covered with roses in summer. The Smiths purchased the house from a descendant of Joshua Paine, the original owner, and have a land grant dated 1731 which came with the house. Six rooms sharing four baths are available for guests, plus two cottages, efficiency and studio in the rear (the old carriage house and stable).

15 Tremont St., Provincetown, MA 02657; (617) 487-1551. Rates are inexpensive. Children are welcome; no pets, please. Parking is available. Open April 1 through October.

Twelve Center Guest House. Captain Josiah Snow built this mansard-style white house in 1872. It's on a quiet, tree-lined street once known as "Money Hill." The Snow family owned the place for more than 100 years. Roger Baker and Jon Richardson, the current owners, enjoy showing off the architectural points of interest such as a graceful center staircase, bay windows and 14-foot ceilings. Each of the eight large guest rooms is simply but attractively furnished, each done in a different color scheme. Two baths are shared. A pleasant efficiency cottage on the grounds is also available. Guests are invited to use the living room and patio; coffee is served each morning and ice is always available.

12 Center Street, Provincetown, MA 02657; (617) 487-0381. (Between Commercial and Bradford streets.) Rates are moderate, lower off season. Visa and MasterCard are accepted. No children under 18 and no pets, please. Parking is available. Open all year.

The Baker House. A typical Cape Cod cottage built in the late 1700s, Mrs. Alice B. Baker's guest house offers a delightfully homelike atmosphere. She has three upstairs guest bedrooms, one single, one double and one large twin, sharing one bath with shower. The house is furnished with some antiques and handmade rugs, and both house and spacious grounds (with a lovely garden for sitting and sunning) have often been painted by artists. Located on a quiet residential street, Baker House is within a three- to five-minute walk of Provincetown's shops, restaurants and beaches. No food is served, but Mrs. Baker provides a hot pot (and supplies) for making coffee or tea.

34 Pearl Street, Provincetown, MA 02657; (617) 487-0614. Rates are inexpensive. No children or pets, please. Parking is available. Open May–October.

Somerset House. Jon Gerrity's Somerset House was built around 1850 by Stephen Cook, a wealthy ship chandler. In the 1890s, new owners doubled its size; it is named after a British frigate which sank off Provincetown in 1778. A pleasant piazza is an excellent place to relax and watch the summerfolk go by—the big yellow house is smack in the middle of town, 100 feet from the town beach. The thirteen large guest rooms, and the rest of the house, too, are beautifully and distinctively furnished. Some rooms are done in period style with Victorian marble-topped furniture; others have a splashingly modern decor. Plants and flowers abound inside and out; walls are heavily hung with paintings. All but one of the bedrooms have private baths. There are also two apartments, each with two bedrooms.

378 Commercial Street, Provincetown, MA 02657; (617) 487-0383. (At Pearl Street.) Rates are moderate, lower off season. Minimum stay for Memorial Day weekend is three days, seven days for July 4 and Labor Day weekends. Visa and MasterCard are accepted. Well-behaved children are welcome; no pets, please. Limited private parking available, plus a public lot across the street. Open April 1–December 1.

Sandpiper Beach House, Provincetown, Massachusetts

Sandpiper Guest House. The Sandpiper, owned by Charles E. Mehr, is a nicely-maintained white Victorian beach house on Provincetown's main street. It is right on the beach, with thirteen light, bright guest rooms, all but two with private baths. Some rooms have balconies overlooking the water; others face Commercial Street, and still others have private ground-level entrances facing the beach. The rooms are furnished in antiques, plus wall-to-wall carpeting. For relaxing, guests have the use of a large lounge/living room, a spacious sundeck, a private beach and swimming pool.

165 Commercial Street, Provincetown, MA 02657; (617) 487-1928. (At Center Street.) Rates are moderate, slightly higher on holiday weekends when a three- or seven-day minimum stay is required. All major credit cards are accepted. No pets, please. Free parking available on premises. Open all year.

The Cape Codder. This large, attractive guest house, a 19th-century Cape Cod with later additions, has thirteen rooms for guests. Most have one double bed, some have two. Five baths, plus a separate shower, are shared. The front upstairs room, the nicest, offers a view of the water. Accommodations also include a luxury apartment recently added to the Bradford Street wing. The Cape Codder is a simple, no frills kind of place with a comfortable, relaxed air and a friendly personal touch. It's located in the East End, a mile from the center of Provincetown, two blocks from several fine restaurants. There is a private sandy beach, with a sundeck, just across the street. Guests are encouraged to bring bicycles for exploring the trails running through the Cape Cod National Seashore Park. Barbara Mayo is your hostess; she and her husband, Stormy, are both marine biologists; he is the chief scientist on the whale-watching boats out of Provincetown.

570 Commercial Street, Provincetown, MA 02657; (617) 487-0131. Rates are moderate, lower off season. Quiet children are welcome, small pets by special permission. There is ample parking. Open mid-April–October.

Dunham Guest House. The original Captain Dunham commanded a whaling ship which was lost off Cape Hatteras in a bad storm. His home, a nice old Victorian, is now owned by Mrs. Alice Dunham—her late husband grew up in it. She runs it with the help of her son and two grandsons. There are four guest rooms sharing one large bath, plus an apartment and efficiency. The rooms are all large and comfortable with long windows and period furniture, including a heavy carved mahogany bed and marble-topped bureau brought back from Jamaica by Captain Dunham.

3 Dyer St., Provincetown, MA 02657; (617) 487-3330. (Prior to May 30, reservations may be made by calling Mrs. Dunham collect at (203) 342-3909 or writing to her at 370 Main Street, Portland, CT 06480). Rates are inexpensive. Children, depending on age, are welcome; no pets, please. Parking is available. Open May 30 through Labor Day.

Victoria House. Whimsical Victorian fripperies and masses of greenery highlight Victoria House. It's about 120 years old, and has four single and five double rooms, plus a double efficiency. Each room is done differently, with brightly-painted walls, period furniture and lots of original prints and drawings. Several refrigerators are available for ice and for keeping soft drinks or beer. Outdoors a porch and small garden are popular places to sit in warm weather. A continental breakfast of coffee, tea or hot chocolate and toast, included in the rates, is provided in season and served in the garden. Len Paoletti, proprietor, says that in the summer his guests are "mixed, gay and straight, and on occasion more gay than straight. But all are welcome; many of the straight guests seem to enjoy the exposure to the other lifestyle. All part of being a tourist."

5 Standish Street, Provincetown, MA 02657; (617) 487-1319. Rates are moderate, lower off season. MasterCard and Visa are accepted. No children as a general rule, but exceptions may be made; no pets, please. No free parking is available; town and private lots are within one block. Open March 1–November 30.

The Capricorn. Located in the peaceful and historic West End of Provincetown, the Capricorn is a very attractive old house, built around 1830. There are twelve guest rooms, five with private bath, all large and tastefully furnished. Guests are invited to use the comfortable living room with color TV and private bar; bring your own bottle and Don Graichen, host and manager, will supply complimentary mixers and ice. A continental breakfast is also "on the house," served each morning in the lounge from 9 to 11. A pleasant sundeck overlooks the bay, and guests often broil lobsters and steaks on the patio.

6 Cottage Street, Provincetown, MA 02657; (617) 487-0959; (winter) (617) 232-8306. Rates are moderate, lower off season. One week's stay is required for July 4 and Labor Day weekends. Open May 15–September 30.

Richmond Inn. Another handsome old house in the West End, this is a sea captain's home dating from the mid-1800s. Authentically restored, it is furnished in period style. Outdoors are a sundeck and lovely gardens for guests to enjoy. The twelve bedrooms, sharing five baths, face either the water or the gardens. James Hay Richmond and James Pardy, owners, serve their guests a continental breakfast in season, included in the rates.

4 Conant St., Provincetown, MA 02657; (617) 487-9193. (On the harbor just west of town center.) Rates are moderate, lower off season. Open all year.

BREWSTER/BARNSTABLE/SANDWICH

From Provincetown, retrace your way on Rte. 6 to Orleans, then pick up Rte. 6A west. Some of Cape Cod's prettiest towns are located along the north shore, including Brewster, Barnstable and Sandwich. The Cape Cod Museum of Natural History, on Brewster's main street, makes an interesting stop especially if you have youngsters with you. Other attractions in Brewster are the Stony Brook Mill, a working replica of America's first grist mill, and Sealand of Cape Cod (just west of town), with playful dolphins and sea lions.

A few miles further, you'll come to the attractive villages of Yarmouthport and Barnstable. Barnstable's salt marshes once supplied salt hay for early settlers' cattle. Sandwich, almost at the end of 6A, is an exceptionally charming village with a picturesque pond and several restored mid-1600s buildings including a working grist mill. Also visit the famous Sandwich Glass Museum where more than 3000 examples of the brilliantly-colored glassware made between 1825 and 1888 are on display.

The Old Manse Inn. In Brewster on Rte. 6A, travelers will find an unusually beautiful guest house—an early 19th-century sea captain's house. A third floor and a mansard roof were added to the original structure in later years, but the old widow's walk remained. In wintertime when the trees are bare, it offers a fine view of the bay. The building has been a guest house since the 1940s, when it was operated by a Lutheran minister's wife (who named it The Manse). In those days, church services were held in the sun room every Sunday.

Doug and Sugar Manchester purchased The Manse in the late 1970s, restored it, and reopened it to guests in 1980. They

The Old Manse Inn, Brewster, Massachusetts

have ten guest bedrooms, all double; two have two double beds and two have twin beds. Nine of the rooms have sinks; three have private baths and the others share baths. The rooms are delightfully decorated with period wallpapers and attractive furniture including many antiques and colorful old quilts. Guests may also use the spacious, comfortable living room and paneled sun room, where stereo, TV, books and magazines, games, cards and card tables are available. The grounds are lovely, with gardens and many trees including several grand old chestnuts. An old barn is currently undergoing restoration.

The Manchesters offer guests a continental breakfast featuring homemade breads, muffins or coffee cake, included in the rates, served in the elegant dining room. Glasses, ice and a refrigerator are provided. The Manse is a half mile from beaches, bicycle paths, tennis and most of Brewster's sites of interest. Restaurants, antique and gift shops are within walking distance.

1861 Main Street (Rte. 6A), P.O. Box 833, Brewster, MA 02631; (617) 896-3149. Rates are moderate, lower off season. Visa, MasterCard and American Express are accepted. Children are welcome, but must be supervised by parents; no cots or cribs are available. No pets, please. Open all year.

The Lamb & Lion. Ken Moore is your host at this handsome guest house in Barnstable, also on Rte. 6A. The main house, an old Colonial, was built in 1740. The original barn and loft have been converted into attractive, modern living units and in 1970, four large double rooms (all with private bath) were added for guests, along with a solarium and swimming pool.

Guest Houses

Set on four acres of rolling land, The Lamb & Lion is designed around an atrium, an open central court, the old wing looking out across the pool to the guest rooms and solarium. A lounge with color TV is available for guests' enjoyment, and spacious sundecks offer views of the harbor, dunes and marsh. A fine antique shop on the grounds has selected period American and English antiques including Sandwich glass, furniture and collector's items. Barnstable Harbor with great sport fishing is only two miles away; the village, with restaurants and shops, is one and a quarter miles away.

2505 Main Street (Rte.6A), P.O. Box 511, Barnstable, MA 02630; (617) 362-6823. Rates are moderate. Children are welcome, but teenagers may find the area's recreational facilities limited. Pets are allowed only by prior approval. Open April 1–October 15; rooms are available by the week at special rates during balance of the year.

MARTHA'S VINEYARD

Beaches, miles and miles of them—they are the pride and one of the major lures of Martha's Vineyard. They seem to go on forever, and if you enjoy solitude you can always find a place that's yours alone. The island, seven miles across the water from Woods Hole, is about twenty miles long and ten miles wide. Inland are moors, ravines, forests and a number of freshwater ponds. At Gay Head, spectacular multi-colored clay cliffs tower 145 feet above the surging ocean. Excellent roads (with no stoplights) take the visitor to beaches, swiftly criss-cross the island, or meander leisurely through lovely, hilly countryside past old farms, stone walls and fields of wildflowers.

Bartholomew Goswold visited the island in 1602 and named it after one of his daughters and for the wild grapes which grew so abundantly. They still do. Martha's Vineyard is a quiet, peaceful island for the most part, and the islanders intend to keep it that way. Commercialism is anathema to most of its residents . . . McDonald's hamburger chain once tried to get permission to open a franchise and was foiled.

The Vineyard's major communities are Edgartown, Vineyard Haven (Tisbury) and Oak Bluffs. The other towns are West Tisbury, Chilmark and Gay Head . . . and there is Menemsha, a tiny "up-island" fishing village, authentic and very photogenic.

Edgartown, the county seat since 1642, is pretty enough to be framed, blooming with flowers and dotted with chic shops and restaurants. Its houses are almost all painted white, except for a few done in natural shingles. Back in the days of the whaling fleet, sea captains built many stately homes that are just as handsome now as they were then, with their classic fanlights and roofs topped with widow's walks. Even the Edgartown jail, built in the early 1870s on the site of a storage shed for whale oil, is attractive. A friend once suggested the appealing structure could conceivably be considered one of the town's fine collection of guest houses! Carrying that thought further, he added, "And it's free, more or less. Stay now — pay later." It serves food, too, prepared by the jailer's wife.

Chappaquiddick Island is just off Edgartown; a short ferry ride on the *"On Time"* will take you over for a drive or bicycle ride. It is a beautiful, serene little island of tangly wooded thickets, sweeping marshes and secluded beaches.

Ferries from the mainland dock year-round at Vineyard Haven, a very attractive town with shady, tree-lined, hilly streets. The most heavily populated Vineyard community, Vineyard Haven has around 3000 permanent inhabitants. In summer, its harbor is crowded with boats of every kind. There are a number of excellent restaurants and shops, too. Booklovers will especially enjoy The Bunch of Grapes bookstore on Main Street . . . two spacious floors offer volumes of all kinds including a large selection of island titles.

Oak Bluffs is an odd little place. Ferries dock here, too, in summer. It began as a tent camp run by the Methodist Church in the mid-1800s, later becoming a thriving summer resort. Today, Oak Bluffs is famed for its unusual collection of American Gothic cottages; these quaint "gingerbread" houses look rather like large versions of children's cut-outs, their ornate jigsaw scrollwork painted in bright colors or pastels. In summer regular band concerts are held near the cottages. And the Camp Ground is the scene for Illumination Night, when all the cottages are decorated with Japanese and Chinese lanterns . . . a charming sight.

My own feeling is that Oak Bluffs is, regrettably, a shade tacky, especially along the streets near the harbor. Nevertheless, it's very popular and fine for families, with lots of things for kids to do including taking a spin on The Flying Horses, an 1880s carousel. There are some very nice parks, too, and of course, a fine beach.

Naturally, with all the marvelous beaches so accessible, the swimming is terrific everywhere on the Vineyard. So are surf fishing and sailing, bicycling, bird-watching and celebrity-spotting. Many famous artists, writers and theatrical folk have summer homes here. Lots of people do bring their cars to the island, but it is easy to get around without one, at least in summertime. Shuttle buses run regularly between some of the towns, and bikes and mopeds may be rented. There are several good bike paths, or you may pedal over the island's 80 miles of paved roads.

Ferries carrying both cars and passengers run from Woods Hole and Nantucket. Ferries carrying passengers only run from Hyannis, Falmouth and New Bedford. Since some of the boats dock at Vineyard Haven and others at Oak Bluffs, check to be sure you're taking the right one. Space for cars is booked up weeks in advance in summer, so if you must bring yours try and make a reservation early. Your guest house proprietor will tell you where to call or write.

Martha's Vineyard has a great many guest houses . . . so if you find the ones described full up, check the listing at the ferry terminal at Woods Hole. It's a good idea to call ahead of time, too, as the houses do a brisk business in season. Also, many of them request a minimum stay of several days or a week.

EDGARTOWN

Chadwick House. Located in the center of Edgartown, the Chadwick House was built by one of the town's numerous whaling captains, in 1840. The handsome Greek Revival-style house, owned by Gene and Jean DeLorenzo, offers fourteen large, airy rooms for guests, tastefully decorated in antiques. Eleven of the rooms have private baths; three share a full hall bath. Most rooms in the main house have fireplaces. A luxury apartment for four offers a beamed cathedral ceiling, wide floorboards, two skylights, fireplace, deck and complete kitchen. House guests are invited to use the spacious front parlor plus a smaller second parlor. (The DeLorenzos say that the larger parlor, with its beautiful staircase at one end, is perfect for weddings.) A continental breakfast, included in the rates, is served in the attractive dining room by an open fireplace. Guests are offered juice, coffee or tea, and delicious homemade coffeecake, rolls or muffins. Chadwick House is one block from Main Street and two blocks from the harbor, within easy walking distance of shops and restaurants.

Winter Street and Pease's Point Way, P.O. Box 1035, Edgartown, MA 02539; (617) 627-4435. Rates are moderate to expensive, lower off season. Visa and MasterCard are accepted. Children 12 years and older are welcome; no pets, please. Guest rooms are open all year; apartment is available early spring–late fall only.

The Daggett House. This splendid guest house is one of Edgartown's most historic. Back in 1660, John Daggett, the first tavern keeper on Martha's Vineyard, was fined five shillings for "selling strong liquor." (He was licensed to sell only beer and ale.) On another occasion, Daggett was fined for "suffering a disturbance in his house." When the present Daggett House was built in 1750, the old tavern's Public Room was included—it forms part of the breakfast room on the garden level, now called the Old Chimney Room for its unique beehive fireplace. In later years the house was used as a store and as a boardinghouse for sailors. During Edgartown's great whaling days, Captain Timothy Daggett, owner of shares in several whaling vessels, operated the place as a counting house.

Today, Fred and Lucille Chirgwin own Daggett House, a beautifully maintained weathered-shingle structure set on a green expanse of lawn and gardens. They also own Daggett House II, an early 19th-century whaling captain's home across the street. The two buildings contain twenty-four double rooms and one single for guests, plus several kitchenette apartments. (In winter only seven double rooms are available.) All have private baths. Also, a charming Garden Cottage on the grounds may be rented.

Beyond the lawn a sea wall encloses a large private sandy beach for guests to enjoy. Lawn games are available, or guests may simply relax and watch the harbor scene beyond the Daggett House pier from under shade trees or lawn umbrellas. Indoors there's a large living room with TV and a library. A full breakfast, included in the rates, is served to house guests in the Old Chimney Room which overlooks the harbor. In addition to the marvelous fireplace, the room includes candlelight doors, a brass flintlock blunderbuss, Betty lamps and a secret staircase! Guests are offered juice, homemade breads and jam, cereal, eggs, French toast or pancakes, and tea or coffee.

North Winter Street, P.O. Box 1333, Edgartown, MA 02539; (617) 627-4600. Rates are moderate to expensive, lower off season. MasterCard and Visa are accepted. Children are welcome; no pets, please. Open all year.

Guest Houses

Point Way Inn. Linda and Ben Smith are the owners of Point Way Inn in Edgartown, a dignified old whaling captain's home opened to guests for the first time in 1980. The Smiths discovered Point Way during the summer of 1979, when they moored their ketch in Edgartown Harbor. They and their two daughters had just completed a 4000-mile, year-and-a-half cruise. Their first winter in the Federal-style house, which was built in 1830, was spent putting in bathrooms, shopping all over New England for antiques, selecting period wallpapers, moving parts of the house and tearing down others. Now they have twelve beautifully appointed double rooms for guests, each with its own bath and ceiling fan. Seven of the rooms have the original fireplaces. In addition, a two-room suite, with fireplace, is available in season.

Guests are invited to enjoy the living room/library, with fireplace and tape deck. A wet bar with refrigerator and icemaker are available. And outdoors, a spacious lawn offers a regulation croquet course and an airy gazebo, where afternoon lemonade is served in summer. The Smiths provide a continental breakfast, included in the rates, of freshly-squeezed orange juice, homemade breads and muffins, and coffee or tea. Breakfast is served in a sunny room opening onto a small enclosed garden. In winter, afternoon tea is served by a crackling fire.

Linda Smith and her family believe in providing guests with all of the nice extra amenities that make one feel pampered: Crabtree & Evelyn soaps and jams, candy from Vermont, stamped envelopes and note cards, pin cushions, scented bureau paper, bedroom carafes and lots of books. Beach towels are supplied in summer, and there is an extra bath where guests may shower after a day at the beach before their boat leaves.

Main Street at Pease's Point Way, P.O. Box 152, Edgartown, MA 02539; (617) 627-8633. Rates are expensive, lower off season. Visa and Master-Card are accepted. Children are welcome; no pets, please. Open all year.

Captain Henry Colt House. A minute's walk from the waterfront, this large white house is located in a quiet area, but right in the center of Edgartown. It was built in 1828 by another of the town's long-ago sea captains. Mrs. Elizabeth A. Berube has six comfortable rooms for guests, with four bathrooms and two half-baths, plus an efficiency apartment for four persons. Visitors are welcome to enjoy the pleasant living room with books, magazines and TV, or relax in the garden. Parking is available right on the premises, and the house is close to restaurants and shops.

North Summer Street, Edgartown, MA 02539; (617) 627-4084. (Next to St. Andrews Episcopal Church.) Rates are moderate, lower off season. Children are welcome; no pets, please. Open all year.

The Victorian, Edgartown, Massachusetts

The Victorian. Another of Edgartown's many whaling captain's homes, The Victorian is located just a block from the harbor. The land was first purchased in 1642, the house built in the early 1700s. Marilyn and Jack Kayner, present owners, have renovated the house's third floor to a period mansard roof with detailed windows and French doors opening onto balconies for water views. They now have fourteen rooms for guests, all with private baths. The rooms, with some antiques including four-poster canopy beds, are tastefully decorated with coordinated wallpaper and linens, eyelet and hand-crocheted dresser scarves and fresh flowers. Guests may use the comfortable sitting room with marble fireplace and TV, and outdoors, an enclosed backyard for relaxing. The Kayners provide guests with a buffet breakfast of fresh fruit in season, homemade preserves, granola, breads and muffins, freshly-ground coffee and English or herb teas. Breakfast, included in the rates, is served in the charming fireplaced breakfast room. *South Water Street, P.O. Box 947, Edgartown, MA 02539; (617) 627-4784. Before April, write or call: P.O. Box 251, Wilmington, VT 05363; (802) 464-3716. Rates are expensive, lower off season. Master-Card, Visa and American Express are accepted. Children are welcome; no pets, please. Open April 1–October 31.*

Guest Houses

VINEYARD HAVEN

The Lothrop Merry House. Built in the mid-1700s, this nice old house was moved from West Chop two miles away to its present location overlooking Vineyard Haven harbor. A typical 18th-century structure, it has a central chimney and six fireplaces. John and Mary Clarke, a charmingly friendly couple, have six double rooms for guests in the house, plus (in season) four more rooms in a cottage annex a short distance away. Three rooms have private baths, three share a bath; the annex rooms also share a bath. Some of the bedrooms have working fireplaces with a supply of wood. Most offer views of the harbor and ocean beyond; the sunrises are magnificent, and at night guests drift off to sleep to the wind-chime sound of harbor bell buoys. All of the rooms are decorated with rag rugs and fresh flowers; one boasts a handsome four-poster canopy bed.

A continental breakfast, included in the rates, offers freshly-brewed coffee, tea and delicious homebaked sweet bread. In the summer breakfast is served out on one of the shady, flower-bedecked brick terraces. In wintertime guests may enjoy their morning repast in the living room/reception area, beside a blazing fire. At the rear of the house, a green lawn with trees, flowers and lawn chairs slopes down to the harbor. The Clarkes have their own sandy beach, with dinghies and sunfish for guests' use. In addition, their 38-foot boat *Irene* is moored in view of the house. It's an authentic 1917 Friendship sloop, and is available for charter by the day or overnight. Host John Clarke, a licensed U.S. Coast Guard captain, skippers the *Irene,* and will take you on cruises among the many coves and small harbors around Martha's Vineyard and the Elizabeth Islands, on evening harbor sunset sails, overnight to Cuttyhunk, or on longer charters to Nantucket.

The Lothrop Merry House is within easy walking distance of Vineyard Haven's restaurants and shops. It's a grand place to visit in summer, but the Clarkes feel that autumn is the best season of all—the water is still warm enough for swimming; boating, biking, tennis and golf are excellent, and for chilly evenings the house's fireplaces warm you up. Even wintertime is pleasant on the Vineyard: the weather is usually milder than on the mainland, many restaurants are open all year, and the beaches are blissfully deserted, ideal for brisk walks or jogging.

Owen Park, P.O. Box 1939, Vineyard Haven, MA 02568; (617)

693-1646. *(Just off Main Street or a short distance along the beach from the ferry dock.) Rates are moderate to expensive, lower off season. Children are welcome; extra cots and port-a-crib are available. No pets, please. Open all year.*

Crocker Guest House. Also located in Vineyard Haven, this is a white Victorian house, built in 1900. Mrs. Kay Whitehead's home is furnished with antiques and is on a quiet, shady street between Main Street and the beach. The ferry, restaurants and shops are only minutes away by foot. There are eight bedrooms, with TV in five. Four have private baths; the others share a bath. No food is served.
Crocker Avenue, P.O. Box 922, Vineyard Haven, MA 02568; (617) 693-1151. Rates are moderate, lower off season. Children are welcome; no pets, please. Open all year.

OAK BLUFFS

Amherst House. Band concerts are played every Sunday evening in summer in the park right in front of this picturesque old house in Oak Bluffs. It is Queen Anne Victorian, built in 1869. Owners Dick Konicek and Marna Bunce (both teachers) aim to make Amherst House as "family" as possible. Antiques fill the house . . . lots of wicker and wood, and a marvelous grandfather clock dating to 1753. There are four rooms for guests, one with private bath. The others, including one with an enclosed front porch offering a great view of park and ocean, share a bath. Guests are invited to use the two parlors, with TV and piano. A continental breakfast of juice, coffee and freshly-baked homemade pastries is served each morning, included in the rates.
38 Ocean Avenue, P.O. Box 644, Oak Bluffs, MA 02557; (617) 693-3430. In winter, phone (413) 367-2020. Rates are moderate, lower off season. Children are most welcome; no pets, please. Open Memorial Day–Labor Day.

NANTUCKET

All islands have a certain appeal, but Nantucket is special. It is my idea of a *real* island, 30 miles out to sea, far removed from sight of the mainland. It's an island of roses, moors and beaches, sunshine and fog, cobblestones and elegant 18th- and 19th-century sea captains' homes.

About fifteen miles long and five miles wide, Nantucket is a small island with a long past. The Indians believed that it was created by a giant, a mighty chief, who tossed a great moccasin-full of sand out into the ocean. Less romantically (except to geologists), it is actually a terminal moraine, a glacial deposit.

The island's largest village is Nantucket Town, settled by Quakers in 1659. For almost a century, from 1740 to 1830, Nantucket was the greatest whaling port in the world. The town retains much of the character of those early days, with its cobblestoned Main Street and collection of serenely beautiful old houses. More than 400 of the homes in Nantucket's historic district have been lived in continuously from the time they were built, in the 1800s and earlier. The oldest of them, the Jethro Coffin House, built in 1686, is open to the public, as are a number of others. And pay a visit to the Whaling Museum, near the Steamboat Authority Wharf—it has an outstanding collection of relics from Nantucket's nautical past.

You will find a wealth of enchanting shops for browsing, and plenty of good places to dine. Like Martha's Vineyard, Nantucket is edged by fabulous beaches, and inland, has miles of rolling green moors. The atmosphere is quiet and decidedly restful; no traffic lights or neon signs disturb the island's tranquility. One doesn't really need an automobile for exploring; many visitors bring bicycles or rent mopeds or bikes and go off by themselves . . . or walk. The less athletic take bus tours. And buses run between Nantucket Town and Siasconset ('Sconset), on the other side of the island.

Nantucket offers a great many guest houses. They are, in fact, the traditional places to stay on the island and there are few other forms of accommodations. Most of the houses are historic, antique-filled and very charming. The ones listed here are a representative sampling. Most are small, however, with a limited number of rooms available, and it's imperative to make reservations as far in advance as possible—especially in summertime. Nantucket Accommodations, an advance reservation service at (617) 228-9559, can be of help if the guest house you choose is full. But even they find it impossible to accommodate everyone at peak times, so do try to plan ahead to avoid disappointment.

Planes fly to Nantucket, and there is a regular car and passenger ferry service from Woods Hole all year. In summer the ferries also run from Hyannis and Martha's Vineyard.

The Periwinkle. Antiques and a harbor view ... the Periwinkle has both. Built around 1846, it is a large house with eleven guest rooms including suites for families. Some have private baths, other share. In addition, a nice old house next door, similar in flavor and style, offers seven more rooms for guests. Owner Sara Shlosser-O'Reilly includes a continental breakfast in the rates—orange juice, coffee and Portuguese sweet bread. Restaurants, shops and the like are within a five-minute walk from the Periwinkle. Your hostess recommends sightseeing Nantucket by bicycle; her house, like most of the others, has a bike rack in the back yard.

7 and 9 North Water Street, Nantucket, MA 02554; (617) 228-9267. Rates are moderate to expensive, lower off season. Children are welcome; no pets, please. Open all year.

Island Reef Guest House. Jane and Ernest Davis feel that their home, built in 1717 and completely restored, is one of Nantucket's most charming. Eleven rooms, all with private baths, are available for guests; all are super-clean and nicely decorated. Guests may also use the Common Room with its traditional Colonial decor. The Island Reef is close to everything—shops, restaurants, beaches and other historic houses.

20 North Water Street, Nantucket, MA 02554; (617) 228-2156. Rates are expensive, lower off season. MasterCard and Visa are accepted. Children over 14 are welcome. Open all year.

Hussey House. Built by Uriel Hussey in 1795, the Hussey House has been carefully restored to retain its original Nantucket air—including the wide floorboards and a fireplace in every room. Furnished with many lovely antiques, the house has six guest rooms, all with private baths, plus some family accommodations. Mr. and Mrs. H. Johnson are the proprietors, and they do make one request: please bring your own beach towels! Hussey House is a few minutes' walk from two beaches, historic Main Street and the docks, and restaurants and shops. Surrounding the house are spacious grounds and gardens for guests' pleasure. In cold weather, visitors are invited to relax around a cozy fire in the sitting room.

15 North Water Street, Nantucket, MA 02554; (617) 228-0747. (Second street on right coming up from dock.) Rates are moderate. Open all year.

Guest Houses

Carlisle House. Built in 1765, this handsome old house is now owned by John and Susan Bausch. Fourteen airy, spacious rooms are available for guests including singles, doubles and one triple; several have private baths, others are shared. They're sparkling clean and decorated in traditional style, some with antique quilts. Guests may also use the comfortable living room and glassed-in porch—where a continental breakfast is served each morning, included in the rates.

26 North Water Street, Nantucket, MA 02554; (617) 228-0720. Rates are moderate to expensive, lower off season. Children over nine are welcome; no pets, please. Open April 1–November 15.

Chestnut House. David and Cathie Belcher own Chestnut House, a charming old structure with a large chestnut tree in its tiny front yard. They have six rooms for guests, three with private baths and three sharing baths, plus a lovely two-room suite with private bath, king-size bed, sitting room and color TV. A separate cottage for four is also available. House guests are invited to use the cozy living room, with TV. Chestnut House is on a quiet, shady side street right in the heart of town.

3 Chestnut Street, Nantucket, MA 02554; (617) 228-0049. Rates are moderate to expensive, lower off season. MasterCard and Visa are accepted. A three-day minimum stay is required in season. No children under five; no pets, please. Open all year.

Cliff Lodge. A gracious old Nantucket home with a widow's walk, built around 1771, Cliff Lodge is owned by Catherine Lynch. There are twelve guest bedrooms including singles, twins and doubles, plus an apartment for two or four persons. Some rooms have private baths, others share. The spacious rooms, and a pleasant parlor where guests may gather, are furnished in antiques. Outdoors, there's a large lawn for relaxation.

9 Cliff Road, Nantucket, MA 02554; (617) 228-0893. Rates are moderate, lower off season. Open May 1–November 1.

The Roberts House Inn. Erected in 1846 as a private residence, this stately Greek Revival building was the home of the Roberts family of Nantucket for almost a century. In 1883 the family opened the house as an inn and it has been welcoming guests ever since. Current owners Sara and Michael O'Reilly have renovated the place to provide more modern conveniences while maintaining the atmosphere of 19th-century Nantucket. There are eleven distinctively decorated, spacious rooms with king- or queen-size beds and private baths, plus several suites for families, also with private baths. In addition, an adjoining building, erected in 1850 for The Society of Friends, offers nine rooms—more simply styled—with private, semi-private and shared baths. A parlor with TV and a large porch are also available for guests' use.

11 India Street, Nantucket, MA 02554; (617) 228-9009. Rates are expensive, lower off season. Visa and MasterCard are accepted. Children are welcome, but only a few at a time. No pets, please. Open May 1 through October.

The House of Orange, Nantucket, Massachusetts

The House of Orange. Orange Street was once known as "The Street of Captains" because of the many Nantucket sea captains' homes lining its old sidewalks. The House of Orange, a typical structure of that period, was built around 1810. Peter Guarino and Paul Willer are your hosts today, and have seven rooms for guests—six doubles and one single. Two have private baths; the others share baths, and some have fireplaces. The house and rooms are handsomely decorated with antiques; guests may also use the large living room and delightful terraced garden. No meals are served, but restaurants are within walking distance, as are shops and beaches.

25 Orange Street, Nantucket, MA 02554; (617) 228-9287. Rates are moderate to expensive. Children over 13 are welcome; no pets, please. Open April 1–January 5.

Guest Houses

Grieder Guest House. Both sides of Mrs. William E. (Ruth) Grieder's family included sea-going men who sailed 'round the world after whales. She is a third-generation Islander and has owned this house for more than 30 years. It was built in the 1700s and is full of Mrs. Grieder's family heirlooms —including pineapple four-poster beds and lovely old quilts. The house, gray-shingled with white trim, has only two guest rooms, so advance reservations are a must. The large twin bedrooms share one modern bath.
43 Orange Street, Nantucket, MA 02554; (617) 228-1399. Rates are moderate. No pets, please. Open May 20–October 1.

The Centerboard Guest House. An elegant old Victorian, Phyllis and Charles Mayhew's guest house in Nantucket's historic district has four double bedrooms, all bright and airy, with semi-private baths. Also a two-bedroom suite and an efficiency apartment with private baths are perfect for families. Guests are invited to use the summer porch, and—off season —the living room. In season, a continental breakfast is included in the rates. Baby-sitting service is available. And Charles Mayhew operates a bicycle rental shop in the same block.
8 Chester Street, Nantucket, MA 02554; (617) 228-9696. (Corner of Chester and Centre Streets). Rates are moderate, lower off season. No pets, please. Open all year.

Corner House. Owned and operated by Jeanne and Bill Walmsley, this is a handsome old whaling captain's home, built in the 1700s. There are five double and twin guest bedrooms with private baths, plus three rooms sharing a bath. Guests are welcome to use the sitting rooms with TV, or relax on the porch and patio. A refrigerator is available for keeping perishables and cold drinks. And guests are offered a continental breakfast, included in the rates.
49 Centre Street, Nantucket, MA 02554; (617) 228-1530. (Across from the Old North Church). Rates are moderate to expensive, lower off season. Children over 12 are welcome; no pets, please. Open all year.

Royal Manor. Leon and Eleanor Royal own the large New England-style house, built around 1850. Set on landscaped grounds, Royal Manor has seven spacious, quiet guest rooms including one single, five doubles and one triple, with private baths. The house is furnished in antiques, old quilts and Ori-

ental rugs, and boasts seven fireplaces. A large open porch and a living room are for guests' enjoyment, too.
31 Centre Street, Nantucket, MA 02554; (617) 228-0600. Rates are moderate. Children over 10 are welcome; no pets, please. Open all year.

Nantucket Landfall. Masses of roses bloom in summer in front of this comfortable, gray-shingled guest house. Mrs. Dorothy M. Mortenson has six rooms for guests, all doubles or triples. Most of the rooms have private baths. The house is directly on the beach, at the harbor. Guests are welcome to enjoy the pleasant living room or sit outdoors on the veranda or lawn. In the morning, complimentary coffee and tea are served.
4 Harbor View Way, Nantucket, MA 02554; (617) 228-0500. Rates are moderate. Open Memorial Day weekend to October 1.

The Carriage House. Once it really was a carriage house; now it's a comfortable, attractive guest house, owned by William and Jeanne McHugh. The architecture is Victorian; it was built in 1865 as part of a whaling captain's estate. Located on a pretty, quiet "country lane," the house is only one block off cobblestoned Main Street. Seven beautifully appointed bedrooms are available for guests, all with private baths. The McHughs provide a complimentary breakfast including home-baked muffins, served outdoors (if weather permits) in a tiny, fenced-in, flower-filled garden. Guests may also use the pleasant living room and game room with cable TV and books.
4 Ray's Court, Nantucket, MA 02554; (617) 228-0326. Rates are expensive, lower off season. Children over 5 are welcome; no pets, please. Open all year.

Phillips House. Another nicely-restored whaling captain's home, Phillips House is about 200 years old. The house is typically Nantucket—full of fireplaces and antiques, with a delightful old kitchen. There are five guest rooms including one with private bath. Mary Phillips, proprietor, serves her guests homemade muffins and coffee each morning, included in the rates. Guests may sit outdoors in the fenced-in patio, with its tiny, colorful garden. The house is a six-minute walk from Main Street.
54 Fair Street, Nantucket, MA 02554; (617) 228-9217. Rates are moderate, lower off season. Open all year.

Guest Houses

Fair Gardens. Claire Murray has an especially deep love for Nantucket; she chose the island as the ideal place to open her English-style bed and breakfast establishment. Fair Gardens was built in the early 1800s; the previous owner was an elderly clockmaker and antique restorer. Claire, who is herself an artist and craftsperson, spent a year restoring the house, making sure the antique flavor was kept intact. Among its many delights are six working fireplaces, and a parlor stove that keeps the kitchen toasty warm on chilly days. A porch and charming brick terrace out back are wonderfully relaxing places to sit; the classic Shakespearean Herb Garden adds to guests' pleasure. On rainy days, books and games are available indoors in the parlor/breakfast room. A continental breakfast with freshly-baked muffins or breads is served each morning, included in the rates.

There are nine guest rooms including doubles, triples and suites, all furnished with antiques. Four have private baths, the others are semi-private, and a few rooms even have fireplaces. In addition, a new three-bedroom house on the property, called the Garden House, offers accommodations for families or two to three couples traveling together. It's available only as a unit, by the week of by the month.

For those readers interested in Colonial crafts, Claire Murray teaches a variety of workshops at Fair Gardens in the spring and fall, including classes in quilting, stenciling, basketry, needle art, rug-making and herbs. She'll be delighted to provide details on dates and other pertinent information. *27 Fair Street, Nantucket, MA 02554; (617) 228-4258. Rates are moderate to expensive. Children are welcome on a limited basis; no pets, please. Open May through October.*

Connecticut

Despite its proximity to New York City, Connecticut is still very much a New England state, historic and very scenic, with many picturesque small Colonial towns. Hartford, the capital, is a bustling insurance center; insurance and industry are the state's major sources of income. But there are lots of farms even today, and miles of tobacco fields stretch along the banks of the Connecticut River.

The land is seventy percent wooded; the landscape ranges from softly rolling hills in the west to lush river valleys in the central region, and finally to the beaches and coastal towns along the Atlantic. Stone walls ramble through fields and alongside roads, and each spring the state's flower, mountain laurel, blooms in delicate profusion.

Connecticut's weather is not as extreme as in northern New England, but the winters can be cold and snowy, especially inland. Along the coast, sea breezes keep visitors comfortably cool in summer. In autumn, the state puts on a typically brilliant New England display of foliage.

Adriaen Block, a Dutch navigator, sailed along Connecticut's coast in 1614. He discovered the Connecticut River, which the Indians called Quonecktacut. Some say that means "long river of the pines"; others interpret it as "long tidal river." Whichever, it certainly is long—the Connecticut starts in northern New Hampshire, forms the boundary between New Hampshire and Vermont, runs down through Massachusetts and then across Connecticut, where it empties into Long Island Sound at Saybrook.

Colonists from Massachusetts arrived in 1634, establishing settlements in the next few years in Wethersfield, Saybrook, Windsor, Hartford and New Haven. In 1638 they drafted a constitution, believed to be the first ever written by a self-governing people. A year earlier they had had problems with the Pequots. The Indians resented the takeover of their land, and killed some of the settlers. The colonists fought back and wiped out virtually the whole tribe.

Guest Houses

In 1687 the British governor-general of the New England colonies, Sir Edmund Andros, tried to end Connecticut's self-rule. He demanded that its charter be surrendered and went to Hartford in person to get it. The wily colonists meekly entered the council chamber and proceeded to debate the matter. Suddenly the lights were blown out and a wild melee resulted—during which the charter was said to have been whisked to a hiding place in a great oak tree. Andros was deposed shortly after that and sent back to England. The "Charter Oak" fell in a storm in 1856; it supposedly was 1000 years old.

Connecticut borders New York State on the west. Rte. 7 runs all the way north into Massachusetts' Berkshire region. Once beyond the Danbury area the route becomes a delightfully meandering country road, following along the scenic Housatonic River much of the way. Western Connecticut also offers several lakes and state forests, good skiing, antique shops galore, and a number of historic, centuries-old towns.

Litchfield, on Rte. 202 east of Rte. 7 (exit at New Milford) is one of the finest surviving examples of a late 18th-century Colonial village. It may have more old Colonial homes still being lived in than any other community in New England. As they *are* inhabited, most are not open to the public, except for Litchfield's annual Open House Day which falls in July, on a different date each year.

Further north back on Rte. 7 you'll come to the Kent area and then to the Cornwalls, a cluster of tiny upland towns surrounded by thickly forested hills. One of the state's few remaining covered bridges crosses the Housatonic at West Cornwall, on Rte. 128 just off Rte. 7.

Connecticut's eastern shore is dotted with attractive villages like Old Saybrook, Old Lyme and Stonington. Just before Stonington is Mystic Seaport, a marvelous living museum of 19th-century maritime America, the adventuresome era of the sailing ships. I-95 runs fairly near the coast between New York and Rhode Island; Rte. 1 does, too, paralleling I-95 in part, but coming closer to the ocean in many areas.

Guest houses, regretfully, have become very rare in Connecticut, more so than in any other New England state. The few that do exist, however, make excellent bases from which to explore—both the surrounding areas and further afield.

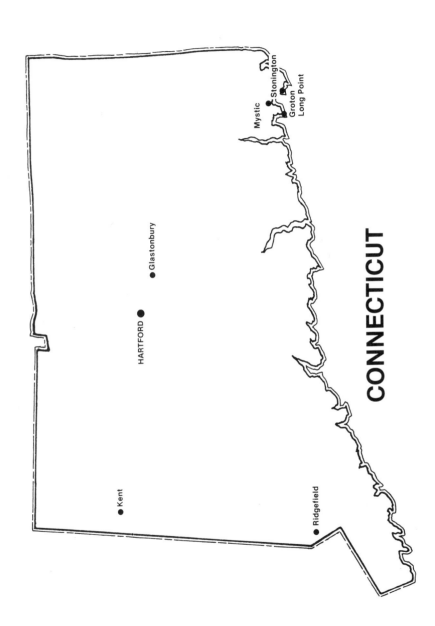

CONNECTICUT

Southwestern Connecticut

RIDGEFIELD

Ridgefield, on Rte. 33 west of Rte. 7, was settled in 1709. A pleasant, tree-shaded town, it boasts many lovely old houses, and is the site of the famous Keeler Tavern, headquarters for Colonial patriots during the American Revolution. The perfectly restored stagecoach inn is noted for a British cannonball embedded in a corner post, lodged there in the battle of April, 1777. The place was operated as a tavern from 1772 to 1907 . . . and nowadays may be toured by visitors. There is a hidden staircase, and outdoors, a charming walled garden. Danbury, a bit north, also has several interesting museums and historic houses.

West Lane Inn. Ms. Maureen M. Mayer is the gracious proprietor of this elegant guest house, located on a quiet, tree-lined street in Ridgefield. A large Colonial, white with black shutters, the house was built in the early 1800s. In the early 1900s West Lane became a hotel/boardinghouse; later it was converted into apartments, and finally into a guest house. There are fourteen spacious, air-conditioned rooms for guests, with queen- or king-size beds and color TV. All are tastefully decorated in traditional style and have private baths, some with bidets. Two of the bedrooms boast working fireplaces, and all include such luxurious amenities as extra-thick towels and blankets. On each landing is a lounge area with comfortable chairs.

Downstairs is a large, attractive foyer with another fireplace and an impressive spindle-type staircase. (Note the handsome woodwork, especially at the top of the stairs.) Guests may use the foyer, relax in wicker chairs on the veranda with its hanging pots of flowers, or sit on the lawn. The house is situated on 1½ acres of beautifully landscaped grounds with many trees, including graceful old elms.

A continental breakfast, included in the rates, is served in a pleasant small dining room or—in season—on the porch. Ms. Mayer will provide a full breakfast if guests wish, at extra cost. The West Lane Inn is close to several fine places to eat (The Inn at Ridgefield is right next door) and also to various area points of interest including the Keeler Tavern. Bicycles may be rented at the house. And there is wheelchair access via a ramp in the back.

22 West Lane, Ridgefield, Ct 06877; (203) 438-7323. Rates are expensive. MasterCard, Visa and American Express are accepted. There's a large parking lot in the rear. Open all year.

Central Connecticut

THE HARTFORD AREA/GLASTONBURY

Connecticut's capital city, Hartford is mainly known for its concentration of insurance company headquarters. History buffs, however, will enjoy the city's many museums and storied old houses. The Butler-McCook Homestead, built in 1782, contains some excellent collections of 18th- and 19th-century furnishings, Chinese bronzes and Egyptian statuettes, plus antique dolls and toys. And Nook Farm offers both the 1874 Mark Twain House (where he wrote several of his books, including *Tom Sawyer* and *Huck Finn*) and the 1871 Harriet Beecher Stowe House. The Wadsworth Atheneum, also located in Hartford, is a nationally renowned art museum with galleries covering every major period.

Glastonbury, just a few miles southeast of Hartford, offers a number of interesting historic homes. Travelers may also enjoy a ferry boat ride across the Connecticut River to Rocky Hill. The ferry, begun in 1655, is the oldest in continuous operation in the country.

Butternut Farm. One of Glastonbury's most historic structures, I'm delighted to say, is today a guest house! Jonathan Hale, son of Samuel Hale, one of the town's important early landowners, was born in 1696. When he married in 1717, he inherited a large tract of land from his father on which he built this house, around 1720. The farm stayed in the Hale family until 1840 when a descendant purchased the *Alert*, a whaling vessel made famous by Melville's *Moby Dick*. Sadly, a mutiny aboard ship combined with an unsuccessful whaling voyage lost both ship and house to creditors.

Today, Donald B. Reid owns Butternut Farm and has four double rooms for guests, one with twin beds and three with four-poster double beds. Two baths are shared. The rooms are appropriately furnished with period pieces, including hand-woven bedspreads and other items from Reid's collection of antiques. You'll be entranced by the house's fascinating architectural features including the large summer beams in the first- and second-story front rooms, wide floorboards, and handsome original paneling and sheathing in every room. Especially appealing is an oversize fireplace with rear bake oven in the north front room. An 18th-century portrait of Jonathan Hale looks down upon a gateleg table surrounded by bannister-back chairs and other period accessories.

Don Reid is also an herb grower and designer of herb gardens. He maintains his own large herb garden on the property, along with another garden near the barn that produces flowers, vegetables and herbs. The house's fireplaced keeping room is bedecked with drying herbs hanging from the ancient beams, and you may purchase some to take home.

A continental breakfast, included in the rates, is served to guests each morning.

1654 Main Street, Glastonbury, CT 06033; (203) 633-7197. Rates are moderate. Children are welcome; pets are not generally accepted. Parking is available at the house. Open all year.

Northwest Connecticut

THE KENT AREA

The town of Kent is located in northwest Connecticut, on scenic Rte. 7. Kent Falls State Park offers a spectacular 200-foot cascade with a path to the top of the falls, picnicking and recreation facilities. Swimming is available in nearby Lake Waramaug; in winter there's skiing at the Mohawk Ski Area further north. At the Sloane-Stanley Museum, travelers will find an outstanding collection of early American crafts and domestic tools, many dating from the 17th century. The ruins of the old Kent iron furnace, part of Connecticut's 19th-century iron smelting industry, may also be seen on the grounds.

Candlelight Tourists. An exceptionally attractive guest house, Candlelight Tourists is located on Rte. 7 in Kent, on the right-hand side of the road if you're traveling north. It's a white, Early American-style house with a spacious front hall, set on lovely, wooded grounds. Mrs. Albert R. Edwards is your very gracious hostess, and has four comfortable, nicely decorated rooms for guests. One room offers a double bed and two singles, two have one double and one single bed each, and one room has twin beds. Guests share a full bath and shower, plus a powder room.

The house, bright and shining clean, was built by Mrs. Edward's husband in the late 1940s. Once their children had left the nest, Mrs. Edwards decided there was a need to provide overnight accommodations for travelers in the area—especially for parents of students at Kent and South Kent, two prestigious preparatory schools nearby. Since then, she has welcomed guests from all over the world!

No food is served, but there is a good coffee shop in a small shopping mall down the road, and a fine selection of excellent restaurants in the vicinity, some within walking distance. In warm weather, guests are invited to relax on lawn chairs outdoors, and the Edwards will be delighted to offer suggestions as to other activities and interesting things to do in the region. *Main Street (Rte. 7), Kent, CT 06757; (203) 927-3407. Rates are moderate. Children are welcome; no pets, please. Parking is available at the house. Open all year.*

Eastern Connecticut

MYSTIC/STONINGTON AREA

Mystic is a nice town all by itself, but Mystic Seaport is fabulous. It is located on the banks of the Mystic River; a century ago it was the site of a bustling shipyard. Today the museum is really three areas: the shipyard, the restored village and waterfront, and various exhibit buildings.

You can wander in and out of a ship chandler's, a sail loft, a hoop shop, a tavern, a newspaper office, drug store and many other structures typical of a busy 1800s seaport community. One of my favorite exhibits is the collection of old carved ships' figureheads, which include a number of handsome, weathered, grand ladies of the sea.

There are, of course, scads of boats to see, more than 200 craft . . . including the last of the wooden whaling vessels, the *Charles W. Morgan*, built in 1841. A Gloucester fishing schooner may also be explored from stem to stern, the *L.A. Dunton*, once part of the sailing fleet that fished on the Great Banks.

Guides called "interpreters" are on hand to explain what is going on. And plenty is—there's a long list of daily events ranging from sail setting and furling, whaleboat demonstrations, steamboat cruises and chantey singing. It's all fascinating . . . a salty trip back in time. Plan to spend half a day at least, more if possible. If by some chance you arrive in late afternoon, your ticket will be validated to include the next day as well, for a small additional fee.

At Christmastime the Seaport celebrates with colorful Lantern Light Tours—a guide carrying a lantern leads visitors to a number of houses, shops, ships and exhibits. The interpreters demonstrate old Christmas customs, including cooking holiday foods on an open hearth. And the entire Seaport is bedecked with Christmas greenery and old-time decorations.

Mystic Seaport is on Rte. 27, which runs off of I-95. Rte. 27 also connects with Rte. 1 if you happen to be following that. Not far from the Seaport is Olde Mystick Village, actually a small shopping center. But it's all in an 18th-century Colonial setting, with more than forty picturesque little shops and restaurants.

Submarine fanciers can stop in nearby Groton and go through a World War II sub, the USS *Croaker*. Bus tours will take you through the U.S. Naval Submarine Base, and a boat tour in summer cruises down the Thames (pronounced Thames) River past the submarines and other points of interest—such as the U.S. Coast Guard Academy in New London. Visitors may also wander about the academy's campus on foot. New London, by the way, has an old cemetery dating to 1653 with the enchanting name of "Ye Ancientest Burial Ground." Ferries to Block Island leave from New London, as well as from Rhode Island ports.

Right on the water, Stonington is another of Connecticut's picturesque 17th-century towns, settled in 1649. It is just off Rte. 1 on 1A, only a few miles from Mystic. Indians fought the colonists here in the early years. Stonington was a thriving shipbuilding village in the old days, and has an active fishing fleet today. The Stonington Historical Society is housed in Whitehall, a beautifully restored country mansion. The Old Lighthouse Museum has an excellent display of whaling gear and ship models, among other intriguing exhibits. One of the nicest aspects of Stonington is its untouched air. It is a quiet, serene little town, not at all "touristy," its streets lined with charming, old (but very much lived in) homes.

For an interesting side trip, drive over to the Gillette Castle State Park in Hadlyme. It's off Rte. 82, on the east bank of the Connecticut River. From Mystic, the shortest route is to follow I-95 south to Old Lyme and then Rte. 156 north to intersection with Rte. 82, and turn left. Or, if you want to avoid major highways, check your map and pick your own route over various country roads.

William Gillette was one of America's greatest actors, famed for his portrayal of Sherlock Holmes. He was a native of Connecticut, and in 1913, he decided to build a home . . . a dream house, as it were. The site, atop lofty ridges of rock amid wooded hills, has a superb sweeping view of the river and surrounding countryside.

The Castle took five years (and more than a million dollars) to build—a sort of medieval fortress with thick granite walls. Some of the furniture was built in; other pieces slide on metal tracks. There are twenty-four rooms in all, a rather haphazard sprawl notable for the actor's attention to the smallest detail—and what may have been a somewhat whimsical mind. Or possibly, a monumental ego.

But Gillette didn't stop there. He constructed his own man-sized railroad outdoors, with a depot near the front entrance and a three-mile stretch of track wending its way through forests and glens. Unfortunately, the railroad has long since been dismantled. The Castle, and its very attractive grounds, are open from Memorial Day to Columbus Day.

**1833 House,
Mystic, Connecticut**

1833 House. A traditional New England guest house, the 1833 House is located in Mystic—almost next door to the south entrance of Mystic Seaport. It's a comfortable, friendly place operated by Mrs. Joan Brownell Smith. She has one single and two double guest bedrooms, sharing one and a half baths, plus a family unit for four consisting of two rooms with a private bath; all have TV. Guests are invited to enjoy good conversation (and make friends with the family cats) in the pleasant, Victorian-style living room, with color TV. Mrs. Smith will entertain guests with travel slides—but *only* if requested! A continental breakfast, included in the rates, is served daily. Your hostess will be delighted to give directions to the area's many sites of interest and activities, including sightseeing and fishing boats, as well as to many fine shops and restaurants. In season, a courtesy bus runs right past her house to downtown Mystic, Olde Mystick Village, the Mystic Marineland Aquarium and railroad station. Gillette's Castle and Newport, Rhode Island, are only an hour's drive away.

33 Greenmanville Avenue (Rte. 27), Mystic, CT 06355; (203) 572-0633. (One mile south on Rte. 27 from Exit 90 off I-95.) Rates are moderate. Children are welcome. Pets may be left with Mrs. Smith while owners are driving or sightseeing, all day if necessary—and they'll receive lots of tender loving care! Open all year.

Pleasant View Guest House, Stonington, Connecticut

Pleasant View Guest House. This nice old house is located in the historic town of Stonington, right on the harbor. It is a white, two-story structure, built around 1885, with a terrace and lawn out back where guests can sit and watch the boats go by. Mr. and Mrs. Edwin D'Amico, your friendly hosts, have five comfortable rooms for guests, most of them sharing a bath. No food is served, but a number of fine restaurants are within walking distance. You'll enjoy exploring the town on foot; it's the best way to appreciate its classic centuries-old charm.

92 Water Street, Stonington, CT 06378; (203) 535-0055. (Off of Rte. 1; when you call ahead, Mrs. D'Amico will give you more specific directions.) Rates are moderate. Open all year.

Shore Inne. Over on Groton Long Point, a peninsula extending into Fisher's Island Sound just southwest of Mystic, you'll find Shore Inne, a delightful guest house with a spectacular ocean view. Located in a quiet residential area and directly overlooking the water, the attractive old house has been renovated and improved by its present owner, Helen Ellison. She has seven comfortable rooms for guests, nicely furnished and brightened with handmade patchwork coverlets. Three of the rooms have private baths; the other four share two baths. Guests may also relax in the pleasant living room with white wicker furniture and a fireplace, or the combined TV/library/sun room. A homecooked continental breakfast, perhaps with Shore Inne Buttermilk Bran Muffins, is included in the rates and served in the dining room. Your hostess will gladly suggest some good restaurants in the area for other meals. Mystic Seaport, Mystic Marineland Aquarium, Fort Griswold, the Coast Guard Academy and U.S. Submarine Base are just a few miles away. Swimming at private beaches, fishing, sunning, biking and tennis are accessible only a few steps from the front door. Boats may be anchored immediately offshore, and day cruises are also available.

54 East Shore Avenue, Groton Long Point, CT 06340; (203) 536-1180. (From Rte. 1, take Rte. 215, then first left after Yankee Fisherman Restaurant onto East Shore Road. Park in rear off Middlefield Street.) Rates are moderate. MasterCard and Visa are accepted. Children are welcome; no pets, please. Open most of the year; sometimes closed from late winter to early spring.

Woodbine Manor, Newport, Rhode Island

Rhode Island

Although it is the smallest state in the Union, Rhode Island has the most impressive official name ... "The State of Rhode Island and Providence Plantations." It also has a whopping great history—marked by religious dissension, boundary fights and slave running, not to mention smuggling and privateering. Its state bird, inappropriately, is a chicken—the Rhode Island Red. A more fitting symbol is the statue atop the dome of the State House in Providence ... a male figure defiantly holding up a long spear, called "The Independent Man."

Back in 1636, Roger Williams had a serious disagreement over religion with the narrow-minded Puritans in Massachusetts. He was forced to flee to Rhode Island where he purchased land from the Narragansett Indians. Other dissenters followed. But they didn't exactly join hands in peace; it wasn't until 1654 that Williams managed to bring the various settlements together. In 1663 King Charles II granted them a charter. Sir Edmund Andros, that disagreeable Colonial governor who tried to take Connecticut's charter back, attempted the same thing with Rhode Island. He failed in both cases.

Newport, known today for its glorious mansions, started off in the 1600s as a raffish seaport town, popular among pirates and smugglers. Like Boston, it made its money through the triangular system of trading in rum, molasses and slaves. Ships took rum to Africa and exchanged it for slaves. The slaves were sold both to the Southern colonies and to the sugar plantation owners in the West Indies—from whence came the molasses for the rum.

In the 1700s Rhode Island bickered almost continuously with the other colonies over boundaries. The problems were finally resolved more than a century later, in the late 1800s. Rhode Island was not exactly a favorite among the other New England colonies at any time; they considered it a pernicious place, a refuge for nonconformists and heretics.

Even after the Revolution Rhode Island tried to maintain its independence, not from England but from the other colonies. It refused to send delegates to the Constitutional Convention and later rejected the newly-drafted Constitution. But when the government threatened to sever relations entirely with Rhode Island in 1790, its voters finally, grudgingly, ratified the Constitution—by a two-vote majority.

The state's small land mass curves around beautiful Narragansett Bay; its shoreline includes both rugged rock and fine beaches. Twelve miles out to sea lies the famed summer resort of Block Island. Inland are quiet country roads and old, historic towns. It is hilly, although there are no real mountains. And the weather is generally mild year-round.

Providence, the capital, is a nice city—founded and named by Roger Williams. A number of old houses and churches may be toured here, and it is the home of Brown University. Roger Williams is buried in the North Burial Ground.

Rhode Island still has a number of comfortable guest houses, particularly along the coast, including some exceptionally pleasant ones in Newport. And as the state *is* so small, you can use any one of them as a base from which to explore other areas, including Connecticut's coastal regions.

WATCH HILL/WESTERLY AREA

If you're driving along the coast from Connecticut, Watch Hill is a nice place to stop for a visit. It's out on a tiny peninsula, off Rte. 1 on 1A, about six miles south of Westerly. The beaches are great, and from Watch Hill Lighthouse you have a magnificent view of Block Island Sound. It is still very much a working lighthouse; the beacon is visible 13 miles out. The last shipwreck occurred in 1962, when the *Leif Viking* ran aground just a few hundred feet off the light. Its captain, so it was reported, radioed the lighthouse and calmly announced, "You have a ship in your front yard."

The town of Watch Hill is old and serene, cooled by sea winds and very relaxing, with a number of attractive century-old houses. Swimming, sailing, charter boat fishing and surf-casting are all popular things to do. And if you like merry-go-rounds as much as I do, you'll delight in the Flying Horse Carousel. It dates back to the late 1800s and is one of the country's oldest—with those charming carved wooden horses that aren't made anymore.

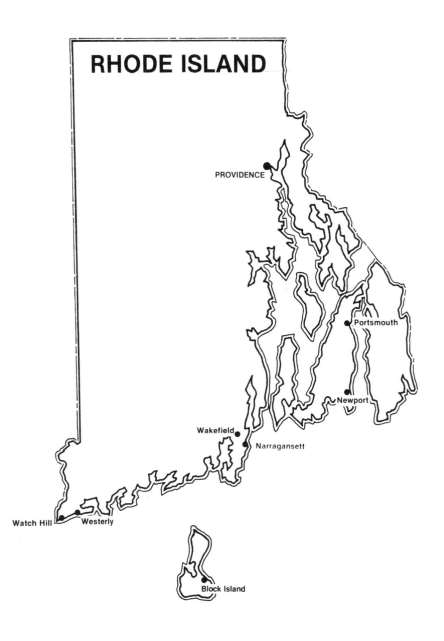

RHODE ISLAND

PROVIDENCE

Portsmouth

Newport

Wakefield

Narragansett

Watch Hill Westerly

Block Island

Guest Houses

Albert Einstein visited Watch Hill one summer in the 1930s. The brilliant physicist turned out to be utterly hopeless at navigating a small boat, according to local legend. Einstein's solution was simple; he set sail each morning and headed due west until he ran aground at sandy Napatree Point. There, some helpful soul would go out and turn him around. Back he'd go—and unless someone leaped into the water and stopped him, he would crash into the dock.

Harbour House. Carole and John Campbell operate Harbour House, located on the edge of Watch Hill Village next to the harbor. The Campbells have three comfortable rooms for guests, all doubles and all with private baths. In addition, there are several apartments and a suite (for six people). The rooms, decorated in simple, homey style, are on the building's second floor. (Downstairs are shops.) There's an outside deck, a great place from which to watch boats sail in and out of the marina. The beach is only a short walk away, for swimming. Harbour House is just twenty minutes from Mystic Seaport in Connecticut, fifteen minutes from historic Stonington.
Bay Street, Watch Hill Village, RI 02891; (401) 348-8998. Rates are moderate. Open mid-May–mid-October, depending on the weather.

Hartley's Guest House. A nice, friendly place, Hartley's is owned by Mrs. Elizabeth Flynn Reilly. It's a large white house with blue trim sitting on a hill overlooking the ocean and Little Narragansett Bay. A porch runs halfway around the outside, with chairs for relaxing and enjoying the view. Your hostess has ten spacious guest rooms, with twin beds. One has a private bath, one is semi-private, and the others share baths. Guests are welcome to use the reading room and watch TV. A breakfast of juice, toast and jelly, coffee or tea is available at a small extra cost. Hartley's is right in the center of Watch Hill Village, two minutes from restaurants and shops, and close to two beaches.
Larkin Road, Watch Hill, RI 02891; (401) 348-8253. Rates are moderate, lower off season. Children are welcome; no pets, please. Open May 30–September 15.

Longvue Guest House on the Pond. Jarvis and Eleanor Alger operate Longvue, an elegant Colonial-style home with spacious grounds. It's not far from Watch Hill, and right on pretty Winnapaug Pond, which is separated from the ocean by

Longvue Guest House, Westerly, Rhode Island

a narrow causeway. The house, white with blue trim, was built in 1946 and is furnished with mahogany and some antique pieces, and Oriental rugs. There are three rooms for guests, one with private bath, two semi-private. In the yard are chairs and umbrella tables where guests may relax and look out over the pond, picnicking and outdoor cooking facilities. Longvue is a mile from the beaches, half an hour from Mystic Seaport and historic Stonington, Connecticut, and one hour from Newport and Providence. Boating, swimming and fishing are available close by. The cordial Algers offer their guests a continental breakfast of juice, toast or buns and coffee for a small extra fee if ordered in advance; breakfast is served, in season, in the pleasant backyard.

Shore Road (Rte. 1A), Box 311, Westerly, RI 02891; (401) 322-0465. (Between Winnapaug and Pond View Golf Clubs overlooking ocean.) Rates are moderate. Children are welcome; no pets, please. Open all year.

NARRAGANSETT/WAKEFIELD AREA

Narragansett is further along the coast, on Rte. 1A off Rte. 1, right where Rhode Island's coastline begins to curve upwards and around to form Narragansett Bay. Newport is over on the other side of the bay. From Point Judith at the tip of the peninsula, ferries leave daily in summer for Block Island. Fishing and swimming are both highly recommended, as is the town—commonly called Narragansett Pier. It has been a summer resort for many years, not as grand as it once was but still most inviting.

Guest Houses

Sea Gull Guest House. Mr. Kimber G. Wheelock, proprietor, welcomes guests to the Sea Gull with certain, not at all unreasonable, exceptions: "The loud and obnoxious will please not bother. We turn away the obvious drunk." Now if you feel that you qualify as a guest, he adds that the Sea Gull is a block away from one of New England's most beautiful beaches, and there are loads of inexpensive things to do in the area. The house is close to restaurants, antique shops and summer theater. The Block Island boat is only ten minutes away, Newport twenty minutes. Excellent offshore fishing is within walking distance. There are seven rooms for guests sharing two baths, one with a giant clawfoot tub, the other with a shower. And, Mr. Wheelock notes, "Guests cannot hear the resident ghost as often since the insulation was blown in." One final word from your host: "Licit and illicit sex are treated about the same."
50 Narragansett Avenue (Rte. 1A), Narragansett, RI 02882; (401) 783-4636. (Call between 5 and 9 p.m.) Rates are moderate, lower off season. No pets, please. Open all year.

Sargent's Guest House. Located in Wakefield, not far from Narragansett, this is an old New England-style house with a huge front porch and many interesting touches inside, such as a fine mahogany bannister. Owners Kathy and Tom Swink are slowly renovating the place, one room at a time. To date they have also insulated and re-sided the house, making it comfortably warm in winter and cool in summer. Each of the seven guest rooms is spacious and individually decorated; three have private baths, two share a bath. Sargent's is on the quiet edge of town, but close to shops and restaurants. Several fine beaches are nearby, offering both surf and sheltered swimming, and the surrounding countryside is lovely.
173 Main Street, Wakefield, RI 02879; (401) 783-1022. (From Rte. 1 take Pond Street Exit; follow Pond Street north to Main Street; Sargent's is on the corner.) Rates are moderate, lower off season. No pets, please. Open all year.

NEWPORT

A grand old summer colony, Newport was founded in 1639. The first settlers were from Massachusetts; then came Quakers from England. In 1658 a number of Jewish families arrived from Holland. The Touro Synagogue, oldest in America, is now a national historic site.

During the American Revolution Newport was occupied by the British for two years. Its fame as a summer watering place for the very, very rich began after the Civil War. Many of the mansions they built are open to the public, and are truly breathtaking.

One of the simpler establishments is Hammersmith Farm, where Jacqueline Bouvier married John F. Kennedy. Built in 1887, the 28-room shingled "cottage" is set on fifty rolling acres of pastures, lawns and gardens. The estate was used in filming the movie "The Great Gatsby,"as Robert Redford's home. Lots of Kennedy memorabilia are on view.

Chateau-Sur-Mer, a gorgeous example of lavish Victoriana, was built for William S. Wetmore in 1852. It has a delightful children's toy museum, in addition to its other charms. Cornelius Vanderbilt's "The Breakers" is located out on Ochre Point Avenue, overlooking the Cliff Walk and the ocean. Richard Morris Hunt designed the structure to resemble a 16th-century Italian palace. With its seventy rooms and stunning grounds it is Newport's grandest. And Marble House, completed in 1892 for another Vanderbilt (William) is named for its sumptuous use of many kinds of marble. Stanford White designed Rosecliff, after the Grand Trianon at Versailles.

Belcourt Castle, built for Oliver Hazard Perry Belmont, is another Richard Hunt extravaganza. It was styled after King Louis XIII's palace in France; Europe's finest craftsmen and artists were brought over to work on the sixty-room residence—at a cost of about three million dollars. Each room is in a different period—French, English or Italian; the grand staircase is all hand-carved. The stained glass collection is outstanding, but there is also a remarkable collection of armor and one of French furniture, silver, and other priceless objects. This last includes a 23-karat gold coronation coach weighing four tons. In case you're feeling a bit peckish after viewing all these splendors, the tour of Belcourt includes tea.

In mid-July, the Newport Music Festival presents a series of concerts of 19th-century music performed in several of the mansions. later on in the summer are the famed Jazz Festival, held in historic Fort Adams State Park, and an Opera Festival. And all visitors should follow lovely Ocean Drive for its 9½-mile length, or better still, hike along the Cliff Walk. You can see some of the mansions and enjoy the ocean view and rugged coastline at the same time.

Guest Houses

Visit the Touro Synagogue and the Quaker Meeting House, both the oldest in America, and wander through Newport's restored historic district with its superb collection of 17th-, 18th- and 19-century houses. For a dizzying change of pace go watch a Jai Alai game at the Sports Theatre. It's an incredibly fast game—the players climb walls and bounce off the floors as they send the ball flying, sometimes as fast as 180 miles an hour.

Sailing cruises leave from Newport for a couple of hours up to a full day, and the schooner *Bill of Rights* takes passengers along the coast for a week's windjamming cruise. Newport is internationally known as a sailing port—the America's Cup Race (held every few years) turns the town into a wild scene of hotly competing yachting enthusiasts from all over the world.

At Christmas, Newport puts on a full month of activities, with concerts, house tours, pageants and bazaars. There is an elegant medieval mass at St. George's School Chapel in near-by Middletown, and a Candlelight Tour of Newport's historic district, a Festival of Trees, a "Traditional Stirring of Christmas Plum Pudding," and much more.

"Wayside." It's not quite as large as the famed Newport mansions, but the "Wayside" is a very handsome house indeed. It is a mellow brick, turn-of-the-century home built for the Elisha Dyer family. Later it was used as a dormitory for a local college, and now belongs to the Post family. Mrs. Dorothy Post, a charming and gracious lady, feels that Newport is a great place to visit at all seasons of the year. She will be delighted to tell you about everything there is to see, and recommend good restaurants and antique shops, too.

"Wayside" has six rooms for guests in the main house, plus a fully-furnished apartment for two couples or a family in the Carriage House. All the large, comfortable, bed-sitting rooms have private baths and are individually decorated. Some have queen-size beds, others doubles or twins. For indoor amusement, guests are invited to use the pool table, play games, read books and magazines or watch TV. Outdoors there's a swimming pool. Coffee and pastry are yours each morning, at no charge.

"Wayside" is located on Bellevue Avenue, near the mansions and the Cliff Walk. Beaches and tennis courts are both nearby—you can even play a tennis game on grass courts at the International Lawn Tennis Hall of Fame! Or you may rent a bike, moped or sailboat for exploring.

Bellevue Avenue, Newport, RI 02840; (401) 847-0302. (Between Parker and Narragansett Aves.) Rates are moderate, lower off season. Children are welcome in the Carriage House; no pets, please. There's plenty of space for parking, even for boat trailers. Open all year.

Bella Vista Guest Manor. Bella Vista's owners, Alice C. Simpson and Rosamond Hendel, have been offering visitors to Newport a genuinely warm welcome for many years. Their guests come from all over the United States, Canada and Europe, and have included such famous personages as pianist Hazel Scott, tennis star Pancho Segura, and actors Charlton Heston and Gypsy Rose Lee. Miss Lee even wrote part of her book *Gypsy* here.

A twenty-room "cottage," Bella Vista was built before the turn of the century for Governor Franklin of Pennsylvania, in the style of an ancient Irish castle. Today it retains much of its old-world character. The white-shingled house, furnished with many lovely antiques, is surrounded by spacious grounds, with lots of green shrubbery and tall shade trees. A long, open veranda with wicker chairs provides a delightfully restful atmosphere. Bella Vista is located in a quiet residential area on the Cliff Walk, but is close to antique shops, boutiques and restaurants, as well as many of the palatial estates and other Newport attractions. Bicycles may be rented nearby, and fishing, tennis, Jai Alai, surfing and swimming are easily accessible. (Please bring your own bath towels.)

There are ten rooms suitable for two or more persons, with semi-private baths and extra powder rooms, and a suite of three rooms for two or four with private bath and kitchen. All of the rooms are unusually large and airy, with modern, comfortable beds.

1 Seaview Avenue, Newport, RI 02840; (401) 847-4262 or 846-7330. (Take America's Cup Avenue into Memorial Blvd., up the hill seven blocks to Cliff Ave. Turn right on Cliff and go two short blocks to Seaview Ave. Bella Vista is the large three-story white house on the corner.) Rates are moderate, lower off season. Your hostesses are sorry, but they cannot accommodate children or pets. There is free parking on the grounds. Open most of the year.

Guest Houses

Woodbine Manor. This elegant guest house is located right in the heart of Newport's old historic district, above the harbor. Built around 1832 in Greek Revival style, Woodbine Manor was originally the fashionable summer home of the wealthy Eckeley family of South Carolina, and reflects the graciousness of the antebellum South. The main stairway, which follows the flow of a curved wall, is lit by stained glass windows designed by Newport artist John LaFarge. The tower on the front of the house was added in the late 1800s for a view of the harbor, and a more recent addition is an impressive columned portico over a stepped, brick patio (the former columned porte-cochere). Berenice Wood is your hostess at Woodbine Manor; her family has owned the house since 1874. She's directly descended from John Howland of the *Mayflower*; her family crest was granted to John's father, William Howland, in 1543 by Queen Elizabeth I.

The house is furnished in Victorian and Edwardian styles, with Early American and Oriental antiques. There are four very large guest rooms: one single and one double have private baths, the others share a bath. From Woodbine Manor it's only a short walk to the famed Touro Synagogue and Trinity Church, and the harborfront with its restored Brick Market and attractive boutiques, antique shops and excellent restaurants. The beach is eight minutes away; fishing and boating are easily accessible.

82 Mill Street, Newport, RI 02840; (401) 846-3538. Rates are moderate. There's free parking just across the street. All of the guest rooms are open from April–November; a few are available all year.

The Queen Anne Inn. Peg McCabe welcomes guests to her charming Newport house, of Queen Anne Revival architecture built in 1890. Situated on one of the town's most historic streets, the house is only two blocks from the waterfront. There are ten attractively decorated rooms for guests, with period wallpapers and furnishings. Included are one single, eight doubles and one triple, with five shared baths. Guests may also use two comfortable lounges, a small second-floor porch, an exterior porch, and a delightful little patio and garden. A continental breakfast, included in the rates, is provided each morning.

16 Clarke Street, Newport, RI 02840; (401) 846-5676. (Two blocks from the harbor, off Washington Square.) Rates are moderate. No pets, please. On-site parking is available. Open all year.

Yankee Peddler Inn, Newport, Rhode Island

The Yankee Peddler Inn. Also located in Newport's historic district, the Yankee Peddler was built in the 1830s as a private residence. Today, the place belongs to Mr. Don C. Glassie Jr., and he has twelve large double rooms plus three one-bedroom suites for guests. Two of the rooms have a shared bath; the others have private baths. Each room is individually decorated, furnished with antiques, and boasts a fireplace. Guests are invited to use the spacious lounge area, which can accommodate small groups for meetings or seminars. A continental breakfast of juice, coffee and pastry, included in the rates, is served every morning in the breakfast room. The Yankee Peddler is a short walk from the harbor, the shopping district, and many of Newport's historic sites and houses. Beaches, mansions and the Ocean Drive are a few minutes away by car.

113 Touro Street, Newport, RI 02840; (401) 846-1323. (Between Washington Square and Bellevue Avenue.) Rates are moderate to expensive. MasterCard, Visa and American Express are accepted. Parking is available. Children are welcome; no pets, please. Open all year except for the month of February.

PORTSMOUTH

Portsmouth is a historic old town not far from Newport. In the 1630s, Anne Hutchinson settled here for a time. Another of the religious liberals banished from Boston, she was tried and convicted on the charge of "traducing the ministers." An interesting place to visit in Portsmouth is the Prescott Farm and Windmill House on West Main Road, a group of restored buildings which include a working windmill, circa 1812. The windmill still grinds cornmeal which is sold at the adjacent country store, built around 1715.

General Richard Prescott's guardhouse contains furniture from the Pilgrim period in its museum. General Prescott, by the way, was commander of the British forces in Rhode Island. His rule came to an ignominious end in 1777 when the Colonials captured him one night—in his nightshirt.

Also in Portsmouth, on Cory's Lane, are the enchanting topiary gardens called "Green Animals." The gardens were started around 1880 and now have eighty sculptured trees and shrubs, beautiful formal flower beds and vegetable gardens. The "animals" are droll creatures, all carefully manicured into amusing shapes by clever gardeners.

Twin Spruce Tourists. Twin Spruce, owned by Mrs. D. C. Ferreira, is a comfortable Colonial-style house set on spacious, well-kept grounds with many trees and shrubs. The surrounding land includes historic Fort Butts, scene of a Revolutionary War battle. Mrs. Ferreira, who hooks handsome heirloom rugs, has four pleasant rooms for guests, sharing three baths. Guests may also use the living room with TV or the nice outside porch with lawn chairs. Your hostess serves complimentary coffee and toast in the mornings if desired. Restaurants and shops are nearby, and Newport is only a short drive away. *515 Turnpike Avenue, Portsmouth, RI 02871; (401) 683-0673. (200 feet from stoplight; Rte. 114 on Mt. Hope Bridge Road.) Rates are moderate. Well-behaved children are welcome; no pets, please. Open all year.*

BLOCK ISLAND

The island's original inhabitants were the Narragansett Indians —they called it "Manisses," or the Isle of the Little God. The Florentine explorer Verrazano discovered it in 1524, and Adriaen Block, for whom it is named, landed there in 1614. English settlers came to the island in 1661.

Today, Block Island is a breeze-swept little summer haven seven miles long and three and a half miles wide. Vacationers began enjoying its peaceful solitude back in the 1800s, and still come in droves each year. Ferries take you to the island from Newport, Point Judith and Providence, Rhode Island, and from New London, Connecticut.

It's a delightful place, with all the charm one expects from an island—rolling moors, miles of stone walls, sandy roads, many small lakes and ponds, and lots of beaches. From Mohegan Bluffs, clay cliffs rising 185 feet from the Atlantic, one commands a spectacular view of the ocean and distant shore.

Visitors may swim or sunbathe on the beaches, bicycle or hike, pick wildflowers and watch birds, go surf or deep sea fishing, or just sit around and be lazy in the comfortably cool salt air. And you don't really need a car.

The Guest House. The Guest House, also called Holiday Haven, is owned by Mary and Derry Johnston. Built in 1903, the house is a spacious Victorian, with wide lawns and a marvelous ocean view. The atmosphere is informal, quiet and relaxing. There are five rooms for guests. One bath is shared and three of the rooms also have their own washbasins. Guests are welcome to use the pleasant living room. No food is served, but Mrs. Johnston sometimes offers morning coffee. Restaurants are within a short walking distance, as are marinas, docks and beaches.

Center Road, Block Island, RI 02807; (401) 466-2676. Rates are moderate; a two-night minimum stay is requested. Open mid-June to mid-September.

Gables Inn and Gables II, Block Island, Rhode Island

Gables Inn & Gables II. Barbara and Stanley Nyzio Jr., and their two daughters, are your hosts at the Gables—two large, comfortable guest houses located at the end of town near Old Harbor. Built in the 1860s, both structures have been faithfully restored and furnished in turn-of-the-century decor, including old-fashioned wallpaper and antiques. For guests

Guest Houses

there are two single rooms, ten doubles, nine triples and five apartments (the last with fully-equipped kitchens). There's also a separate cottage for rental, with kitchen. Four attractive sitting rooms, with color TV, and several shaded verandas, with rockers, are fine places to relax and socialize with the other guests. The backyard offers horseshoes, croquet, barbecues and picnic tables; beach chairs and towels, barbecue utensils and cook pots are available on request. Tea and coffee are on tap all day, and there are refrigerators for keeping perishables. The Gables are only a minute's walk from restaurants, beaches, stores, churches and theater.

Dodge Street, Old Harbor, P.O. Box 516, Block Island, RI 02807; (401) 466-2213 or 466-7721. Rates are moderate, lower off season. Children are welcome; no pets, please. Open all year.

Index

Note: Guest houses that serve breakfast, either included in the rates or for a small extra charge, are starred. (*)

Guest Houses
(Maine continued)

Massachusetts

Guest Houses

New Hampshire

Guest Houses
(Vermont continued)

ABOUT THE AUTHOR

Corinne Madden Ross, a free-lance writer living near Boston, stays in guest houses whenever possible on her many travels. She has published numerous travel articles and is author of **The Southern Guest House Book** (East Woods Press, 1981), and co-author, along with Ralph C. Woodward, of **New England: Off the Beaten Path** (East Woods Press, 1981).

She is also the author of **To Market, To Market: Six Walking Tours of the Old & the New Boston** (Charles River Books, 1980).

East Woods Press Books

Backcountry Cooking
Berkshire Trails for Walking & Ski Touring
Campfire Chillers
Canoeing the Jersey Pine Barrens
Carolina Seashells
Carpentry: Some Tricks of the Trade from an Old-Style Carpenter
Complete Guide to Backpacking in Canada
Drafting: Tips and Tricks on Drawing and Designing House Plans
Exploring Nova Scotia
Florida by Paddle and Pack
Free Attractions, USA
Free Campgrounds, USA
Fructose Cookbook, The
Grand Strand: An Uncommon Guide to Myrtle Beach, The
Healthy Trail Food Book, The
Hiking Cape Cod
Hiking from Inn to Inn
Hiking Virginia's National Forests
Honky Tonkin': Travel Guide to American Music
Hosteling USA, Revised Edition
Inside Outward Bound
Just Folks: Visitin' with Carolina People
Kays Gary, Columnist
Living Land: An Outdoor Guide to North Carolina, The
Maine Coast: A Nature Lover's Guide, The
New England Guest House Book, The
New England: Off the Beaten Path
Parent Power!
   A Common-Sense Approach to Raising Your Children In The Eighties
Rocky Mountain National Park Hiking Trails
Sea Islands of the South
Southern Guest House Book, The
Southern Rock: A Climber's Guide to the South
Steppin' Out: A Guide to Live Music in Manhattan
Sweets Without Guilt
Tennessee Trails
Train Trips: Exploring America by Rail
Trout Fishing the Southern Appalachians
Vacationer's Guide to Orlando and Central Florida, A
Walks in the Catskills
Walks in the Great Smokies
Walks with Nature in Rocky Mountain National Park
Whitewater Rafting in Eastern America
Wild Places of the South
Woman's Journey, A
You Can't Live on Radishes

Order from:

The East Woods Press
429 East Boulevard
Charlotte, NC 28203